Political Economy of Islam

Series Editors
Hossein Askari, George Washington University, Washington, DC, USA
Dariush Zahedi, University of California, Berkeley, CA, USA

All Middle Eastern countries, with the exception of Israel and Lebanon, profess Islam as their state religion. Islam, whether simply in words or in fact, is woven into the fabric of these societies, affecting everything from the political system, to the social, financial and economic system. Islam is a rules-based system, with the collection of rules constituting its institutions in the quest to establish societies that are just. Allah commands mankind to behave in a fair and just manner to protect the rights of others, to be fair and just with people, to be just in business dealings, to honor agreements and contracts, to help and be fair with the needy and orphans, and to be just even in dealing with enemies. Allah Commands humans to establish just societies, rulers to be just and people to stand up for the oppressed against their oppressors. It is for these reasons that it said that justice is at the heart of Islam. In the same vein, the state (policies) must step in to restore justice whenever and wherever individuals fail to comply with divine rules; government intervention must enhance justice. This series brings together scholarship from around the world focusing on global implications of the intersections between Islam, government, and the economy in Islamic countries.

More information about this series at
http://www.palgrave.com/gp/series/14544

Putri Swastika · Abbas Mirakhor

Applying Risk-Sharing Finance for Economic Development

Lessons from Germany

Putri Swastika
State Islamic Institute Metro (IAIN Metro)
Metro, Indonesia

Abbas Mirakhor
La Junta, CO, USA

Political Economy of Islam
ISBN 978-3-030-82641-3   ISBN 978-3-030-82642-0 (eBook)
https://doi.org/10.1007/978-3-030-82642-0

© The Editor(s) (if applicable) and The Author(s), under exclusive license to Springer Nature Switzerland AG 2021
This work is subject to copyright. All rights are solely and exclusively licensed by the Publisher, whether the whole or part of the material is concerned, specifically the rights of translation, reprinting, reuse of illustrations, recitation, broadcasting, reproduction on microfilms or in any other physical way, and transmission or information storage and retrieval, electronic adaptation, computer software, or by similar or dissimilar methodology now known or hereafter developed.
The use of general descriptive names, registered names, trademarks, service marks, etc. in this publication does not imply, even in the absence of a specific statement, that such names are exempt from the relevant protective laws and regulations and therefore free for general use.
The publisher, the authors and the editors are safe to assume that the advice and information in this book are believed to be true and accurate at the date of publication. Neither the publisher nor the authors or the editors give a warranty, expressed or implied, with respect to the material contained herein or for any errors or omissions that may have been made. The publisher remains neutral with regard to jurisdictional claims in published maps and institutional affiliations.

This Palgrave Macmillan imprint is published by the registered company Springer Nature Switzerland AG
The registered company address is: Gewerbestrasse 11, 6330 Cham, Switzerland

CONTENTS

1	**Introduction**	1
	Medieval Christian Europe and Prohibition of Interest Rate-Based Transactions	2
	Replacing Interest-Rate Contracts	4
	Risk Sharing Finance and German Economic Miracle	7
	Feder's Policy Influence	12
	References	14
2	**The Impact of Risk Sharing for the German Economy**	17
	References	21
3	**Risk Sharing Economy: A Framework**	23
	German Economic Policies: 1933–1935	28
	Epistemology of Risk Sharing in Islamic Finance	32
	References	45
4	**Historical Review of Risk Sharing Instruments**	47
	Risk Sharing Application in Conventional Literatures	47
	Evolution of Public Finance Instrument: Public Finance Instruments in the European Land	68
	Fiscal Instruments in the Ottoman Empire	73
	References	79

v

vi CONTENTS

5 The Foundation of the German Economy: Concept and Practices — 83

Up to the Nineteenth Century — 83

The Early Twentieth Century — 92

The German Economy During the Great Depression — 103

References — 110

6 Risk Sharing Macroeconomic Policies — 113

General Conditions: 1932 to January 1933 — 114

Macroeconomic Policies of the Third Reich: 1933–1935 — 117

Work-Creation Bills (Arbeitbeschaffungswechseln) — 124

Tax Remission Certificates (Steuergutscheine) — 130

Monetary Policy: Policy of Discounting — 133

References — 136

Index — 139

LIST OF FIGURES

Fig. 3.1   Government finance and risk transfer management   25
Fig. 3.2   Government finance and risk sharing management   27

LIST OF TABLES

Table 2.1	GDP Growth of Germany (y.o.y) vis-a-vis the United Kingdom and France	19
Table 3.1	Allocation for jobs creation bills redemption	30
Table 6.1	Economic data (in annual figure)	115
Table 6.2	Unemployment statistics (January 1932–January 1933)	117
Table 6.3	Financing work-creation programs	122
Table 6.4	Estimated & approved plan of work creation program	125
Table 6.5	Projected financial budget of work creation programs on Reich Treasury: 1934–1938 (mil. RM)	127
Table 6.6	Tax remission certificates (Mil. RM): 1932–1934	132
Table 6.7	Interest rates from 1932 to June 1936	135

ix

CHAPTER 1

Introduction

This book is about risk sharing, a concept that has been with humans since their pre-history existence, a way by which humans share the risks of life on earth. Anthropologists suggest that sharing in general has played a crucial role in human history from its very beginning to now. They argue that sharing is the central rule of social interaction among hunters and gatherers who *"represent the oldest and perhaps most successful human adaptation"* (Lee, 1998, p. ix). Studies of contemporary hunter-gatherer societies demonstrate that, by and large, they share the risks and rewards of their activities (see, for example, the collection of such works edited by Gowdy, 1998). These societies conceive of the world as an integrated whole, nature as a sharing partner and their own society as one governed by brotherhood (see, for example, Bird-David, 1998, pp. 123–127). History also shows that until the third millennium, production, exchange and trade were based on risk/reward sharing. Archaeological evidence from the Middle East from eight to third millennium B. C. suggests strongly that risk sharing is a pre-historic concept (see, for example, Mattessich, 1987, p. 71). However, beginning in the third millennium, a new mode of financial transaction appeared in Mesopotamia (Sumeria, Babylonia, Akkadia, and Assyria): risk transfer in form of interest-rate debt instruments (Graeber, 2011). Based on available research, economic historians suggest that interest rate, mechanism of this new mode of

© The Author(s), under exclusive license to Springer Nature Switzerland AG 2021
P. Swastika and A. Mirakhor, *Applying Risk-Sharing Finance for Economic Development*, Political Economy of Islam,
https://doi.org/10.1007/978-3-030-82642-0_1

1

financing, was "invented" by the Sumerians sometimes during the third millennium as reflected in various law codes of the period—such the code of Lipit-Ishtar, the code of Hammurabi, and the Assyrian law code, as available in archaeological finds (Graeber, 2011; Mirakhor & Askari, 2019, pp. 77–82).

Whereas prior to the third millennium, financial transactions and trade were carried out on the basis of partnerships, where risks and rewards (or losses) of ventures were shared, beginning in the middle of third millennium, methods of financing ventures also included debt in which the creditors demanded a fixed rate for the amount they lent over a fixed period of time regardless of the outcome of the venture, thus transferring all the risks of transactions to the borrowers. Soon after the "invention" of interest-rate mechanism and its associated modes of financial transactions, a radical form of risk transfer appeared in which risks of a bilateral transaction were shifted to third parties without their knowledge or consent (Cizakca, 2014; Mirakhor, 2018). An example of risk shifting is a form of debt-slavery occurring when a debtor defaulted on a debt and, consequently, the creditor took the debtor's family as slaves.

A contemporary example of risk shifting was observed in the aftermath of the 2007/2008 financial crisis when financial institutions were bailed out and the costs were shifted to the taxpayers. In today's situation, this pandemic will lead to debt crisis and inherits its burden to younger generation.

MEDIEVAL CHRISTIAN EUROPE AND PROHIBITION OF INTEREST RATE-BASED TRANSACTIONS

With a few exceptions, these two modes of financing have co-existed from the third millennium B. C. to the present. The exceptions appeared in Muslim countries, in Medieval Europe, and in Germany, 1933 till the end of WWII. In latter instances, interest-rate mechanism was prohibited based either on religious belief or based on national economic policy priority. Both in Muslim countries and in Medieval Europe, interest rate was prohibited as it was seen as unjust. Church Fathers, such as Saint Augustine (354–430 AD) and Saint Jerome (342–420) prohibited any transaction based on "usury"; a term defined as a financial transaction in which the lender requires the borrower to repay more than the sum borrowed. Saint Augustine defined a usurer as one who in a debt contract expected an amount larger than the principal loaned. Similarly, Saint Jerome defined usury as any excess beyond the principal loaned (see McLaughlin, 1939; Nelson, 1969; Noonan, 1957) thus indicating an arithmetic equivalence between the notion of usury in Christianity and modern "interest rate" charged on debt. As Noonan (1957, p. 15) indicates, this equivalence meant mandated equality between the principal loaned by the creditor and its payoff by the lender. Church Fathers' position on the impermissibility of interest-bearing debt contract was founded on theological ground based not only on the Old Testament which forbad it but also on the New Testament in which Jesus commands: "Lend freely, hoping for nothing therefrom" (Luke 6:35).

The logical foundation of Christian scholars' defense of prohibition of usury was strengthened substantially in the Medieval period as they gained access to Aristotle's thoughts through the intermediation of Muslim scholars whose books had become available to European scholars in the eleventh and twelfth centuries. In the first three centuries after the advent of Islam, Muslim scholars had developed elaborate logical arguments explaining the prohibition, mandated by the Qur'an, relying partly on Aristotelian logic. Medieval Christian scholars, known as "Scholastics" whose methodology of research and argument held sway in Europe from the twelfth until the seventeenth centuries, found the Muslim Aristotelian scholars' arguments in support of the prohibition in consonance with the Fathers' theological arguments (Grice-Hutchinson, 1952; Langholm, 1979; Mirakhor, 2014). The latter had defined sin as perversion of order. Aristotle had made a distinction between a natural order in which money served as a medium of exchange only and an acquisitive order in which money's role was misdirected and used as means of accumulating wealth through usury. Aristotle had argued that money is barren and cannot regenerate itself through usury. This would be an "unnatural birth." In effect, Aristotle argued that the creditor's demand for additional amount beyond the principal constitutes an unnatural claim since it is a demand for something that does not and cannot exist.

Scholastics' arguments relating to the prohibition of usury was firmly anchored on their primary concern for social Justice. Saint Thomas Aquinas, the most famous of these scholars, argued: "*To accept usury from money lent is unjust itself, for one party sells the other what does not exist, and this manifestly constitutes inequality which is contrary to justice*" (Kaye, 1998, p. 86).The scholastic doctrine also considered usury as theft because the creditor's demand for unjust payments in addition to the principal lent violated the debtor's property rights. Above all, Scholastics were moralists who, guided by scripture, focused on search for rules of justice that govern social interactions. Prohibition of usury was one such rule which was based on doctrines of benevolence, mutual benefits, fraternity and the responsibility of members of society to each other, and the instrumental role of wealth in support of these objectives. In this context, prohibition of usury served distributive as well as commutative justice.

In recent years, some scholars—relying on the axioms of contemporary economics: scarcity, rationality, and self-interest—have reinterpreted the scholastic doctrine of usury. Placing emphasis on the model of "economic man," instead of justice and morality, they argue that the scholastic position was meant to justify rent-seeking activities of the Roman Catholic Church (see, for example, Eckelund et al., 1996). Such a position runs counter to long-standing scholarship that emphasizes the centrality of scholastics' concern with social justice. For example (Dempsey, 1948; Schumpeter, 1954) not only show the strength of scholastics' concern for social justice but forcefully argue the logical validity of their position on usury. Noonan (1957, p. 360) concludes that in the case of scholastic's usury doctrine, *"the theory is formally perfect."* In responding to the new interpretations of scholastic doctrine, Monsalve (2014, p. 216) suggests that the new interpretation "focus in some way the vested-interest dimension of the usury prohibition. A common feature in these new approaches is the emphasis placed on the concept of 'homo-economicus' rationality (utility maximization) over justice and moral concerns. These evolutionary approaches seem to shrink the moral dimension of scholastic economy, which would appear as an ex post attempt to legitimize the particular doctrinal position of the Roman Catholic Church on this matter without seeing much merit in its logical reasoning" (see also Poitras, 2016, pp. 70–76).

Replacing Interest-Rate Contracts

Scholastic doctrines of brotherhood, benevolence, property rights, social responsibility of individuals toward other members of the society, the requirement that transactions between and among parties must be based on mutual benefits through fair and just exchange, use of wealth as an instrument of transfer for meeting the minimum needs of others, their ideal of social justice, all formed the foundation of their doctrine of prohibition of usury. Collectively, these doctrines stressed that humans must share the risks of life on earth and no one had the right to transfer or shift risks to others. Violations of this doctrine had severe penalties. Usurers were excommunicated and not allowed to be buried in Christian cemeteries. Functionally, this meant that alternatives had to be found to replace interest-rate mechanism. In the event, the scholastics relied on "*Commenda*": a mode of financial transaction advocated by Muslim scholars (Nyazee, 1997) as well as another similar mode: Roman "*societas*." The latter was defined as "*a union of two or more combining money or skill for the purpose of making profit*" (Kaye, 1998, pp. 82–83; Poitras, 2016, p. 77). It was made clear that while the share of the profit for each of the participants would be negotiated at the beginning of a commercial venture, the percentage of the profit could not be fixed ex anti as a percentage of the capital invested (Poitras, 2016, pp. 80–87).

Fourteenth and fifteenth centuries witnessed the beginning phase of changes in and strengthening of both risk sharing and risk transfer; trends that continued well into the eighteenth century. During the latter period, another major evolutionary innovation in form of "*limited liability corporation*" which placed a cap on the obligations of corporations, changed the essence of both methods of managing the risks of finance. Risk sharing evolved from partnerships employing *commenda*—in which risks and profits of ventures were shared in accordance with the terms of an ex anti contract—to "*Joint-Stock Companies*." Poitras (2016, pp. 109–185; Pryor, 1997) traces this evolution and explains the history of development of early Dutch and English joint-stock companies in Europe. These companies were formed to finance significantly large ventures for long distance trade with much greater equity capital and larger shareholders than partnerships. As Poitras indicates, in the following centuries, economic and legal changes permitted these companies to evolve into limited liability corporation with autonomous, exchange traded shares (Gonzalez de Lara, 2002; Poitras, 2016, p. 157; Schmitthoff, 1939). Concurrent with the evolution of risk sharing finance, views of Europeans on permissibility of interest-rate financing (risk transfer) changed as well (Nelson, 1969). This evolution had its beginning in the fourteenth century and picked up momentum to make interest-rate debt fully acceptable by the nineteenth century. Soon this sort of debt became a significant part of the capital structure of firms.

Along with legal developments, changes in the organizational form of businesses—most important of which were the limited liability and the separation of ownership and management—had far reaching impact on entrenching risk transfer as the dominant form of finance and facilitating empowerment of risk shifting (Cizakca, 2014). The most significant consequence of these changes was the growth of informational problems such as asymmetric information and moral hazard (Mirakhor, 2018). As these changes were taking place, economics and finance disciplines were shedding their moral and ethical moorings to the point to allow a prominent economist to suggest that "economics is not a morality play" and another to argue "finance has no moral flag to fly." Morality-free "science" of economics and finance provided intellectual support for risk transfer and risk shifting finance. But the dominance of interest rate-based debt imposed huge costs as it renders economies and their financial systems unstable, prone to recurrent crises. As Reinhart and Rogoff (2009) demonstrate, all financial crises over "eight centuries" have been "debt crises" (Askari et al., 2021, pp. 3–45).

Aside from huge costs of recurrent crises, the design, operation, and maintenance of a debt system imposes significant costs on the taxpaying public. These costs are most often hidden and not subject to scrutiny. Most people are not aware that debt system is not naturally stable and lacks the incentive structure to make it self-sustaining. It requires a supporting system of laws, legislation, an edifice of complex administrative enforcement structure in terms of courts, lawyers, police, and, in number of countries, means of incarceration for defaulting on debt. These are some of the running costs of operating an interest-rate debt system of finance in the budget of governments along with interest payments in the debt servicing costs. These costs are ultimately financial burdens on the members of society through taxation. As explained by contract theory, the main reason for these costs is that a debt contract is an example of a class of contracts called "impossible contracts." Given the axioms of economics—scarcity, rationality and self-interest—the borrower has no incentive to repay the principal, much less the interest on debt, and therefore the lender has no incentive to lend. From the time of Sumerians, it has been recognized that to make these contracts possible, a large system of third-party enforcement is needed. Nevertheless, and even with full operation of enforcement system, interest rate-based debt systems remain unstable and fragile (Mirakhor, 2018). The reason is that, at their core, debt contracts cannot include provisions for truth telling, malfeasance, excessive risk taking and other behaviors that affect the borrowers' ability to repay the loan. The hidden costs of enforcement of impossible debt contracts are in effect free insurance provided to creditors; its costs are shifted to taxpayers. Debt systems also promote rentier economies, create and empower income and wealth inequality (Akin & Mirakhor, 2019; Piketty, 2014, 2020) and undermine social solidarity.

Risk sharing contracts, on the other hand, are fundamentally stable, have no costs to third parties, are efficient in terms of reducing costs and increasing output (X-efficiency and allocative efficiency), and have positive impact on reducing income and wealth inequality (Akin & Mirakhor, 2019). Moreover, risk sharing based economies are not only stable but have the potential to be antifragile (Taleb, 2012, 2018), meaning that their strength is enhanced in the face of crises (Rafi et al., 2016; Rafi & Mirakhor, 2018). The key reason is the fact that participants in a risk sharing contract have "skin-in-the-game" and that creates sufficiently strong incentive for all parties to ensure the success of the venture (see Taleb, 2018). Positive attributes of risk sharing and the negative aspects of risk transfer financial systems are not known to the general public and are not studied sufficiently by researchers to create a ground swell of support for implementation of fully risk sharing economy and finance. This is true even in Muslim countries where the dominant religious belief requires implementation of such systems (Mirakhor & Askari, 2017; in this context, see also Abdulkarim et al. (2020) for the role of debt and financialization in contemporary Muslim countries). However, a single experience in the twentieth century that attempted—and to a large degree succeeded—to implement such a system was Germany. It is the contention of this book that the speed of the recovery of the German economy 1933–1935 and its rapid resumption of economic growth, termed *"miraculous,"* owed much to adoption of risk sharing paradigm. In turn, this adoption was due to the persuasive arguments of one thinker: Gottfried Feder.

Risk Sharing Finance and German Economic Miracle

It is not unusual to read books and articles about the history of German economy between the wars and its recovery from a near total collapse—suffering from unbearable war-reparation, high unemployment and hyperinflation—without much reference to the important paradigm shift in financing that took place in 1933–1935. As upcoming chapters of the book indicate, the change in financing in a symbiotic relation with job-creating initiatives laid the foundation for emergence of a solid, stable, debt-free economy with near full employment and little or no inflation by 1935, before the start of rearmament program. Whatever else is credited (or blamed) for these developments, it is certain that substantially reduced reliance on interest-based debt finance played a highly important role in the German economic miracle. This role has not been given the attention it deserves. Hence, the ways and means by which the German economy's reliance on debt financing gave way to financing by widespread risk sharing among all participants in the economy is the focus of this book.

Mostly ignored are also the thoughts of Gottfried Feder inspired by Silvio Gesell and arranged by Hjalmar Schacht, the originator of the central idea that the tyranny of a debt-based system was, in the main, responsible for the impoverishment of the German economy and society. When his name is mentioned in any book or article about the history of German economy before WWII, he is quickly dismissed (see, for example, Silverman, 1998, p. 49). It is seldom mentioned that he had known Hitler, had been the latter's mentor and influenced Hitler's economic thinking as well as those of the National Socialist German Workers' Party (NSDAP).His genius has seldom been recognized (see, however, Schenk & Bromley, 2003 for an exception). This is particularly unfortunate because his economic arguments against risk transfer and risk shifting finance are unique to an age seduced by interest rate-based finance. The main reason may be the fact that he combined his valid arguments against debt finance with despicable racists ideas that shortened the shelf life of the logic and cogency of his economic arguments in support of an interest-rate-free economy.

Feder's economic arguments for replacing a debt-based financial system with a risk sharing paradigm appeared in his book: Manifesto for the Abolition of Enslavement to Interest on Money, published in 1919. Economic analysis in this book focused on the causes of the impoverishment of the German economy and ways and means of addressing its economic ills and restoring economic growth and stability. After presenting his economic arguments, Feder devotes a large portion of his book to responding to all possible objections to the program for recovery and resumption of economic growth of Germany in detail with proofs for his arguments drawn from actual data on the German economy (Manifesto, pp. 43–53). His arguments against "interest-slavery" and his assertion that the wealth of a nation was represented by its labor power and its productive capacity and not in gold and foreign exchange reserves constitute the focal points of his thesis. He insisted that when faced with high unemployment and hyperinflation and no gold and no foreign exchange, German government needed to take control of its monetary and fiscal policy to create conditions for full employment. These points constituted the core of the economic program advocated by the National Socialist German Workers' Party (NSDAP).

In His Manifesto, Feder combined succinct economic arguments, data from the German economy, and passionate rhetoric to make the point that unless societies and their economies liberate themselves from "enslavement to interest," they would continue to suffer unacceptable and growing income and wealth inequality[1] class conflict, social, economic and financial instability, and impoverishment. He began his analysis by presenting his conception of "*Mammonism*" which he considered as the backbone of money-based "global order." This order, he asserted, derives it immense power from "interest on loans." Loans he divided into "*loan capital...the curse of all laboring humanity*"—with infinite, insatiable power of growth through compound interest with power to transfer and shift all risks to borrowers and third parties—and "Industrial capital" (or productive capital through risk sharing). The latter's growth he saw as orderly and finite, never exceeding the growth capacity of the society since the source of returns to this capital was finite amount of profits from productive activities.

Mammonism[2] he conceived as a system and as a mindset. He argued that: "Mammonism is the heavy, all-encompassing and overwhelming sickness from which our contemporary cultural sphere, and indeed all mankind, suffers. It is like a devastating illness, like a devouring poison that has gripped the peoples of the world." As a system, he defined Mammonism as a "supragovernmental financial power enthroned above any right of self-determination of peoples…" As a mindset, Mammonism "has taken hold of the broadest circle of peoples; the insatiable lust for gains, the purely worldly-oriented conception of life that has already led to a frightening decline of all moral concepts and can only lead to more.

---

[1] See also Piketty (2014, 2020) who argues that rents (including interest earnings) are the main cause of the growth of inequality in contemporary societies.

[2] See Stewart Davenport (2008) for an interesting view of how the early American Christian economists mobilized their intellectual abilities to create an argument for the compatibility of Christianity and Mammonism.

This mindset is embodied and reaches its acme in international plutocracy" (Manifesto, p. 7). A "blindness" has been created by this mindset such that people cannot "see clearly that the doctrine of the sanctity of interest is a monstrous self-deception..." This illusion has "entangled our entire thinking in the golden web of international plutocracy" to the point that even the ordinary people with some surplus funds which they loan do not realize that the interest earned from these funds "are completely offset by taxes." Ultimately, he argued, these taxes are "only a tribute-obligation to big capital, and not, as we would imagine, a voluntary sacrifice for the accomplishment of labor for the community." He concluded that a change in the mindset of people could also change the system of Mammonism through "liberation from enslavement to interest on money" which becomes "the clear motto for global revolution, for the liberation of productive labor from the chains of supragovernmental money-power" (Manifesto, pp. 10–20).

His arguments against the interest-rate mechanism took on an Aristotelian color in that he fundamentally questioned the ability of money, in and of itself, to create more money. Thus, he argued that money is only "*a slip of paper...Nothing, nothing at all, can come from money alone.*" He reminded his readers that throughout history only the efforts of human beings have been responsible for progress of humanity. This progress "*has been made not by money but by the men themselves, their bold spirit, their proud daring, their clever minds, the strength of their hands, their shared, therefore social, industrious labor.*" He saw the role of money as a mechanism that facilitated exchange. His economic explanation echoed a long held philosophical tradition that argued only labor power—mental and physical—is capable of creating value, not money. Thus, argued Feder, "*only after people have sensibly agreed on the facilitation of the exchange of goods for consumption, to write vouchers for completed labor, only with that does the slip of paper receives meaning and purpose...But with that the power of money should end.*"

In his Manifesto, Feder offers a nine-point program—encompassing his views on money, banking, capital, macroeconomic policies, employment, and income—as follows: (i) conversion of all debt instruments to risk sharing instruments; (ii) removal of interest from all debt servicing contracts; only principal were to be repaid with periodic repayment; (iii) real estate debts were to be freed from interest; (iv) all real estate credit were to be extended under full control of the central bank; (v) monetary system and policy were to be placed under the direct control of the central bank; (vi) payments of dividends on equity were to be limited to no more than 5% of the annual profits; beyond this, the residual profits were to be distributed to "risked capital" (equity), as an incentive to increase in equity capital; (vii) interest payments on existing debt contracts were to be pooled and distributed "as pension" to those unable "to earn their livelihood"; (viii) earnings from war-debt instruments issued by the state were to be subjected to "strongly graduated tax," and existing wealth was to be subjected to a "flat-rate tax"; and, finally (ix) money was to have only the role of medium of exchange; a massive public education program was to propagate the principle that money should never be granted "*a supra mundane power to grow of itself by means of interest, at the expense of productive labor*" (Manifesto, pp. 8–9).

The nine-point program, once implemented, Feder asserted, will put an end to the exploitation of the economy by finance which he did not see as facilitating production, employment and trade but as means of empowering the elite, global, rich banking community that dominated world finance. Eliminating the interest-rate mechanism he saw as the only solution that could end German economy's crises and allow it to stabilize and resume its growth in short order. He was adamant in his belief that removing the interest-rate mechanism and thereby eliminating or at least reducing the power of "loan capital" would channel financial resources to "industrial capital." That is channeling funds to equity capital rather than debt capital. This, in turn, would increase employment and income. Feder's prediction that by disempowering interest-rate mechanism German economy would recover and resume its growth was validated in a short period of two years, 1933–1935. Without belaboring these points further, it suffices to say that even a cursory reading of Feder's writings on the adverse impact of interest on the society and its economy, as well as the necessity of eliminating this mechanism of debt-slavery, makes clear that Feder's main concern was the injustice of the operations of this mechanism. In that sense, Feder's position is continuation of the views of religious scholars as well as non-religious moralists throughout history that interest constitutes an instrument of creating and sustaining growth of injustice in human societies. In both systems of thought—religious and moralists—the focus is on the unity and brotherhood of humans and the necessity of sharing the risks of life. Both religious thinkers and the moralists have rejected the idea of shifting or transferring risk of transactions to the second or third parties without their knowledge or consent or under duress.

Among the religions, the most comprehensive position on injustice is held by Islam (Askari & Mirakhor, 2019; Mirakhor & Askari, 2019) including its unequivocal position on the injustices involved in the operations of the interest-rate mechanism. As the next chapter shows, this position is clearly stated in the Qur'an. The latter warns of economic, social and spiritual impoverishment of societies that allow the operation of this mechanism. It is important at this juncture to emphasize that this book deals with the intersection of the teachings of Islam and those of the thinkers and policymakers of Germany before WWII, represented by Feder, on the damages that interest-rate mechanism brings to a debt-based economy and society that relies this mechanism. The attempt is to demonstrate the positive results of eliminating this mechanism and relying on risk sharing finance—what Feder called "industrial capital"—for economy and society in a contemporary, complex and industrial economy such as that of pre-War Germany. The central motivation of doing so is to respond to those who regard Islamic finance as a fourteen-century old system that may have worked in small agricultural and trade-oriented societies but is, by and large, irrelevant to and not applicable to "modern," industrial economies. This is the extent of our interest in the economic thought and history of pre-War Germany. Accordingly, the book does not deal with social policies of Germany. It does not share the reprehensible dimensions of Feder's thought or German government's policies, such as racism, which prevailed during this period.

Feder's Policy Influence

Feder had become a member of the German Workers' Party, before it was renamed as NSDAP, at the same time as Hitler whom Feder mentored for a time. In 1920, NSDAP adopted formally Feder's ideas, summarized in his book: The 25 Points, as its own policy manifesto summarized in the moto: "*The German State on a National and Social Basis*" (Schenk & Bromley, 2003, p. 109). The central proposition of this manifesto was focused on restructuring the German economy as one liberated from "*interest-slavery*" and one in which labor power and its productive capacity determined the value and strength of its currency not its gold or foreign exchange holdings in the national bank. Hitler praised Feder's genius and adopted his economic ideas as his own.

In Mein Kampf, he refers to Feder "as the person who first clarified for him the deadly contradictions and weakness of international capitalism." He explained: "If ever need makes humans see clearly, it has made the German people do so. Under the compulsion of this need we have learned in the first place to take full account of the most essential capital of a nation, namely its capacity to work. All thoughts of a gold reserves and foreign exchange fade before the industry and efficiency of well-planned national productive resources. We can smile today at an age when economists were seriously of the opinion that the value of currency was determined by the reserves of gold and foreign exchange reserves lying in the vault of the national banks and, above all, was guaranteed by them. Instead we have learned to realize that the value of currency lies in a nation's power of production, that an increase volume of production sustains a currency, and could possibly raise its value, whereas a decreasing production must sooner or later, lead to a compulsory devaluation...we were not foolish enough to try to make a currency [backed by] gold of which we had none, but for every Mark that was issued we required the equivalent of a Mark's worth of work done on goods produced" (quoted in Feder, 1919, p. 1).

The resolve to adopt unorthodox ideas of Feder—particularly the need to remove reliance on the interest-rate mechanism in macroeconomic policies and implement work creation initiatives via risk sharing finance—saved the German economy from the depth of depression with hyperinflation and high unemployment. Within a short period of two years the German economy was well on its way to recovery and resumption of economic growth to become the strongest economy in Europe. As Feder suggests, during this period, *"the unemployment problem had been solved and the country was back on its feet. It had a solid, stable economy, no debt, and no inflation, at a time when millions of people in the United States and other Western countries were still out of work and living on welfare"* (Feder, 1919; see also Emry, 1984; Liu, 2005). It is the objective of this book to investigate the ways and means through which the German economy managed to accomplish this major achievement.

While there is no evidence showing that Feder was religious, he did combine his economic analysis with a peculiar moral sensibility (peculiar, given his racism). This book contends that structuring an economy based on risk sharing finance induces economic growth and development even if the society in which the economy is imbedded is not guided by religious beliefs. Because of the nature of the incentive structure associated with the belief in an eternal life and ultimate accountability, however, the institutional scaffolding of a society governed by rules of social and economic behavior prescribed by scriptures enjoys greater stability. The next chapter outlines the risk sharing financial system and its operations in accordance with the teachings of Islam. Some believe however that such a system cannot be implemented in contemporary, complex societies. The later chapters of the book present the operations of a risk sharing system which prevailed in one such economies, the German economy, and show the positive results achieved by Germany in a short period of time from implementing an interest-rate-free economy.

References

Abdulkarim, F. M., Mirakhor, A., & Hamid, B. A. (2020). *Financialization of the economy and income inequality in selected OIC and OECD countries: The role of institutional factors*. De Gruyter.

Akin, T., & Mirakhor, A. (2019). *Wealth inequality, asset redistribution and risk-sharing Islamic finance*. De Gruyter.

Askari, H., & Mirakhor, A. (2019). *Conceptions of justice from Islam to the present*. Palgrave Macmillan.

Askari, H., Iqbal, Z., Krichene, N., & Mirakhor, A. (2021). *Risk sharing in finance: The Islamic finance alternative*. Wiley.

Bird-David, N. (1998). Beyond 'The original affluent society': A culturalist reformulation." In J. Gowdy (Ed.) (pp. 115–138).

Cizakca, M. (2014). Risk sharing and risk shifting: An historical perspective. *Borsa Istanbul Review, 14*(4), 191–195.

Davenport, S. (2008). *Friends of the unrighteous Mammon: Northern Christian & market capitalism, 1815–1860*. The Chicago Press.

Dempsey, B. (1948). *Interest and usury*. Dobson.

Eckelund, R., Herbert, R., Tollison, R., Anderson, G., & Davidson, A. (1996). *Sacred trust: The medieval church as an economic firm*. Oxford University Press.

Emry, S. (1984). *Billions for bankers, debts for the people*. Lord's Covenant Church.

Feder, G. (1919/2012). *The Manifesto for the abolition of enslavement to interest on money*. Translated from German by Hadding Scott. Published by McHenry History.

Gonzalez de Lara, Y. (2002). Institutions for contract enforcement and risk sharing: Rom the sea loan to the 'commenda' in late medieval Venice. *European Review of Economic History, 6,* 257–262.

Gowdy, J. (Ed.). (1998). *Limited wants and unlimited means: A reader on Hunter-Gatherer economics and the environment.* Island Press.

Graeber, D. (2011). *Debt: The first 5,000 years.* Melville House Publishing.

Grice-Hutchinson, M. (1952). *The school of Salamanca: Readings in Spanish monetary history, 1544–1605.* Clarendon Press.

Kaye, J. (1998). *Economy and nature in the fourteenth century: Money, market exchange, and the emergence of scientific thought.* Cambridge University Press.

Langholm, O. (1979). *Price and value in the Aristotelian tradition: A study in scholastic economic sources.* Universitetsforlaget.

Lee, R. B. (1998). Foreword. In J. Gowdy (Ed.), *Limited wants, unlimited means* (pp. ix–xii).

Liu, H. C. K. (2005, May 24). Nazism and the German Economic Miracle. *Asia Times.*

Mattessich, R. (1987). Prehistoric accounting and the problem of representation: On recent archeological evidence of the Middle East from 8000 B. C. to 3000 B. C. *Accounting Historians Journal, 14,* 71–91.

McLaughlin, T. P. (1939). The teachings of canonists on usury. *Mediaeval Studies, I,* 81–147.

Mirakhor, A. (2014). Muslim contribution to economics. In M. Cizakca (Ed.), *Islam and the challenges of western capitalism,* published by Edward Elgar.

Mirakhor, A. (2018). Risk sharing and the systemic fragilities of debt-economy. *Intellectual Discourse, 26*(2), 291–308.

Mirakhor, A., & Askari, H. (2017). *Ideal Islamic economy: An introduction.* Palgrave Macmillan.

Mirakhor, A., & Askari, H. (2019). *Conception of justice from earliest history to Islam.* Palgrave Macmillan.

Nelson, B. N. (1969). *The idea of usury: From Tribal Brotherhood to Universal Otherhood.* Princeton University Press.

Noonan, J. (1957). *The scholastic analysis of usury.* Harvard University Press.

Nyazee, I. A. K. (1997). *Islamic law of business organization: Partnerships.* IIIT

Piketty, T. (2014). *Capital in the twenty-first century.* Harvard University Press.

Piketty, T. (2020). *Capital and ideology.* Belknap Press.

Poitras, G. (2016). *Equity capital: From ancient partnerships to modern exchange traded funds.* Routledge.

Pryor, J. (1997). The origin of the commenda contract. *Speculum, 52,* 5–37.

Rafi, U., & Mirakhor, A. (2018). *Antifragility of Islamic finance: The risk-sharing alternative.* Peter Lang.

Rafi, U., Mirakhor, A., & Askari, H. (2016). Radical uncertainty, non-predictability, antifragility and risk-sharing Islamic financing. *PSL Quarterly Review, 69*(279), 337–372.

Reinhart, C., & Rogoff, K. (2009). *This time is different.* Princeton University Press.

Schenk, T., & Bromley, R. (2003). Mass-producing traditional small cities: Gottfried Feder's vision for a greater Nazi Germany. *Journal of Planning History, 2*(2), 107–139.

Schmitthoff, M. (1939). The origin of the joint-stock company. *University of Toronto Law Journal, 3*, 74–96.

Schumpeter, J. A. (1954). *History of economic analysis.* Oxford University Press.

Silverman, D. P. (1998). *Hitler's economy: Nazi work programs, 1933–1936.* Harvard University Press.

Taleb, N. N. (2012). *Antifragile: Things that gain from disorder.* Random House.

Taleb, N. N. (2018). *Skin in the game: Hidden asymmetries in daily life.* Random House.

CHAPTER 2

The Impact of Risk Sharing for the German Economy

As mentioned in the introduction, historians have documented significant influence of risk sharing in economic development in various parts of the world throughout time. In the Middle East, risk sharing contracts, such as "*modaraba*" and "*musharaka*," were utilized widely by merchants throughout history (Çizakça, 1996). It was common for capital owners, in this region to enter a financial transaction with the entrepreneur under the contract of "*modaraba*" and "*musharaka*." The basis of these contracts was simple. The parties bore the business risk of an economic venture according to the degree of their financial and labor participation in the undertaking. Centuries later during the medieval period European merchants adopted these financing instruments under a different name (de Lara, 2003).[1]

At the macro level, economic historians also found traces of risk sharing principle utilized for public financing (Çizakça, 2006). As early as the seventh century, Islam mandated a risk sharing and redistributive

---

[1] *Modaraba* contract was known as "*Commenda*" in Venice, Genoa, Pisa, and expanding also to the Spanish and French coastal cities. In the German land, the contract was known as "*Fürlegung*" (Southern Germany) or "*Sendegeschäft*" (Northern Germany and Hansa cities). There was also "*Societas Maris*" that resembled the contract of "*Musharaka*."

© The Author(s), under exclusive license to Springer Nature Switzerland AG 2021
P. Swastika and A. Mirakhor, *Applying Risk-Sharing Finance for Economic Development*, Political Economy of Islam, https://doi.org/10.1007/978-3-030-82642-0_2

17

18   P. SWASTIKA AND A. MIRAKHOR

mechanism called "*zakat*" (levy) in Muslim lands.[2] Under "*zakat*," the system endeavored to smooth consumption of Muslims whose physical or social constraints restricted them from accessing resources and markets. In regions of different faiths, risk sharing principle was enacted in form of tithing mechanism. Citizens assigned a portion of their income to for the financing support of less fortunate. In the banking area, *Credit Mobilier*, a French-based, joint-stock bank, integrated risk sharing principle into its activity. Thanks to *Credit Mobilier*, public projects, such as city adornment of Paris and the railway networks in Western Europe, were undertaken for the benefit of people without imposing interest-rate financing on governments and societies.

While the use of risk sharing instruments and contracts, for production, exchange and trade purposes, have been in use in human societies for at least ten millennia, no country in the world had adopted risk sharing as a national policy before the twentieth century. However, in the 1930s, facing devastating consequences of WWI defeat in terms of onerous reparations, huge unemployment and inflation, Germany chose, as a matter of national policy to adopt risk sharing as the principle means of inducing economic recovery and resuming growth. "Miraculously" successful macroeconomic policies of Germany 1933–1935 initiated Germany's comeback from devastation to become a prosperous nation in a brief period. Within three years, Germany was able to increase the national output and improve her labor market conditions. Unemployment dropped significantly; from 6,013,620 unemployed in January 1933 to 2,507,955 in December 1935. Germany's economic outlook, measured by GDP growth, enhanced appreciably compared to other European economic powers like the United Kingdom and France as shown in Table 2.1.

Table 2.1 demonstrates the reason why, even today, the recovery of Germany from deep depression seems highly significant outcome which could be used as an example of highly successful economic development model that could well solve some of intractable economic problems of contemporary economies. Yet, there are few studies explaining the details

---

[2] *Zakat* is an important means in the system of income redistribution in Islam that applies risk-sharing concept. The objective of income redistribution is to reduce intra- and inter-generational risks arising from economic externalities and inequality of accessing resources. *Zakat* system is to redeem these rights, thus cannot be understood as charity/gift from one person to another (Mirakhor, 2004).

Table 2.1 GDP Growth of Germany (y.o.y) vis-a-vis the United Kingdom and France

Source Angus Madison

of the economic program implemented by Germany before WWII, its underlying principles, and the ways and means of its implementation principle.

As part of this program, for example, the *Vorfinanzierung, or "Pre-Financing" system* enabled direct participation by households, private sectors, and financial institutions in financing national programs (known as *Arbeitsbeschaffungsprogram* or Work-Creation program), without exacerbating the government fiscal burden. Most analysis of German recovery attributed it to factors other than the adoption of risk sharing—such as alleged default on War reparations or expropriation of private property or rearmament. Careful analysis of economic data and policies during the 1933–1935 period, however, reveals that none of these factors were evident during this period. For example, moves toward rearmament or expropriation did not occur until late 1936 by which time risk sharing-based recovery and growth were well underway. Thus, national policies that allowed Germany to outperform the economy of other European nations owed much to genuine effort to reorient the economy away from one in which finance was dominated by the use of interest-rate mechanism toward a risk sharing economy.

Upcoming chapters attempt to show that risk sharing principle was implemented in the German macroeconomic policy of 1933–1935 thus strengthen the argument that the risk sharing principle is quite applicable to the modern, complex economy. That said, the most comprehensive model of application of risk sharing. The Book, therefore, argues that the Islamic financial system can and should be adopted in managing national as well as the global financial markets in order to address socio-economic problems, such as unemployment, poverty, and income inequality that currently plagues national and global economies.

Adoption of risk sharing in national economic policy in Germany 1933–1935 brought the country out of depression and provided millions of jobs to its people. Risk sharing monetary and fiscal policies positively affected banking activities and private investments. As well, it created strong coordination between financial markets and the real sector of the economy. The "Pre-Financing" system, operating in 1933–1935, allowed access to financing for entrepreneurs and local governments to undertake public sector infrastructural projects (Schacht, 1967). The "rediscounting policy", in a way, neutralized interest rate mechanism from coordinating activities of the banking system and monetary policy. Fiscal policy avoided excessive public borrowing for the government programs while sustaining a healthy and sound fiscal balance (Gesell, 1915; 1918).

It is worth repeating that the Book does neither discuss nor support the worldview underlying the racist social policies of the Third Reich or its nationalistic, aggressive rearmament policies as it considers them irrelevant to its adoption of risk sharing economic policies during the 1993–1995 period. No doubt that National Socialism did not understand the full social impact of risk sharing on the economy and the society since it violated the philosophical and moral principles which constitute the motivation for its adoption as the core economic and financial policies from 1936 onwards. This the main reason for the decision to focus data only from the first quarter of 1933 to December 1935 to analyze the German macroeconomic policies to explain the key instruments and institutions that helped German economy in its journey from near total impoverishment prior to 1993 to near full recovery and resumption of economic growth in 1935 (Poole, 1939).

The principle of risk sharing in macroeconomic policies was imbedded in a financial structure which allowed risks of development projects to be distributed among members of the society by providing them the opportunity of financial inclusion through access to financial resources (Mirakhor, 2011). This financing inclusion policy deterred transferring or shifting financial risks to a segment of population or the public at large, or providing a particular segment privileges and protection over the others. The policy allowed sharing of risks and rewards of economic activities and discouraged risk transfer or risk shifting. Further, arrangements under this policy provided the needed liquidity and the necessary mechanisms to cushion impact of crises (Schiller, 1936). Accordingly, two instruments of risk sharing—the work-creation bills and tax-remission certificates facilitated public-project financing and job creation during 1933–1935—were issued to households and the financial sector to provide the liquidity needed to expand real sector activities. Thus, savings from households and the financial sector were mobilized to finance private sector investment opportunities with the objective of increasing employment, income and output growth of the German economy.

REFERENCES

Çizakça, M. (1996). *Comparative evolution of business partnerships*. E. J. Brill.

Çizakça, M. (2006). Cross-cultural borrowing and comparative evolution of institutions between Islamic world and the west. In S. Cavaciocchi (Ed.), *Relazioni economiche tra Europa e mondo Islamico, Secc. XIII–XVIII*. Prato.

de Lara, Y. G. (2003). Commercial partnerships. In *Oxford encyclopaedia of economic history* (pp. 480–483). Oxford University Press.

Gesell, S. (1915). *Finanzielle oder Wirtschaftliche Kriegsrüstung*. Möller. Oranienburg.

Gesell, S. (1918). *The natural economic order* (P. Pye, Ed.).

Grebler, L. (1937). *Work creation policy in Germany, 1932–1935*. International Labour Office.

Mirakhor, A. (2004). Islamic finance and instrumentalization of Islamic redistributive institutions. In *Ibn Rushd Memorial Lecture*. Institute of Islamic Banking and Insurance.

Mirakhor, A. (2011). Risk sharing and public policy. In *The 5th International Islamic Capital Market Forum*.

Poole, K. (1939). *German financial policies, 1932–1939*. Harvard University Press. Retrieved from http://dspace.gipe.ac.in/jspui/handle/1/7358.

Schacht, H. (1967). *The magic of money*. Oldbourne Book Co. Ltd.

Schiller, K. (1936). *Zum Wirtschaftlichen Schicksal Europas*. Junker und Dünnhaupt Verlag.

CHAPTER 3

Risk Sharing Economy: A Framework

Risk sharing is the key institution for development. As Cizakca asserts, in Muslim and in Western countries, risk sharing created the fuel needed for the "*commercial revolution*" (Çizakça, 2014, p. 192). Recently, the world has witnessed the success of risk sharing finance in the hands of venture capitalists (Çizakça, 2011, pp. 249–250). Partners shared the risks of their business as well as profits and losses. Partnership reduced the cost of capital mobilization. Thus, providing a significant channel for accelerating investment, inventions, and innovations.

The prohibition of interest rate-based contracts in Islamic finance constitutes the foundation of the risk-sharing paradigm. Islam condemns charging interest because all interest-based transactions feature an act of shifting or transferring risks to the counterparties. As the scholastics argued, risk shifting and transfer features of debt contracts violate the principles of property rights because creditors secure their property claims upfront and transfer the risk of the transactions to the borrowers. This creates inequality among the parties in the transaction. The lender becomes a "rentier," who earns income in the earning of which no work was performed.

As Piketty (2020) showed, it is this rent that leads to accumulation of wealth. Passed down from one generation to next, it has created

---

© The Author(s), under exclusive license to Springer Nature
Switzerland AG 2021
P. Swastika and A. Mirakhor, *Applying Risk-Sharing Finance
for Economic Development*, Political Economy of Islam,
https://doi.org/10.1007/978-3-030-82642-0_3

23

huge economic inequality within and among nations leading to weakening social cohesion, promoting social divisions, class conflicts, racism, xenophobia as well as economic, social, and spiritual impoverishment. In terms of public risk management, risk transfer and shifting system move economic risk to a particular group, with or without the consent of receiving party. For instance, the financial crisis in 2008 has shown the extent to which private decisions could cause society at huge risk. The decision to bail the "too big to fail" financial institutions put the government function, as the public risk manager, in question.

Risk transfer and shifting create an incentive for economic agents to capture laws, regulations, supervision and oversight apparatus of the government over banking, finance and economic activities. Through this capture, risks of private financial decisions are transferred/shifted to third parties, including taxpayers who ultimately bear the costs of failure of private decisions of big financiers but also the costs of bailing them out. As has been demonstrated empirically, more often than not, big wealth-holders and financiers become wealthier after a crisis. Wealth accumulated by the rich have reached obscene levels. A study by Oxfam—an international confederation of 20 organizations—reveals a shocking fact that the wealth of the one percent of the world population is equal to other ninety nine percent (Oxfam, 2016). Risk transfer and shifting management benefit the extreme minority, the rich, at the cost of highest majority.

As depicted from Fig. 3.1, national economic program is financed by government's fiscal policy. There are no difficulties in financing if the budget is in surplus. However, governments face challenges when their budget is in deficit. Under a system of risk transfer and shifting, three options are available. First option is to improve income tax collection commensurate with the expenditures. This policy is likely to increase taxation and other source of government revenue. The second alternative is borrowing, from domestic and/or external creditors. Under this scenario, government issues bonds or debenture certificates to domestic and/or international markets. Borrowing provides governments liquidity faster than taxation, thus, it has become the first option in the menu of conventional financing strategy for governments. A combination of raising taxations and borrowing is the third alternative for government financing.

All of these policies expose society to a greater risk. The first policy option potentially diminishes household consumption and private sector

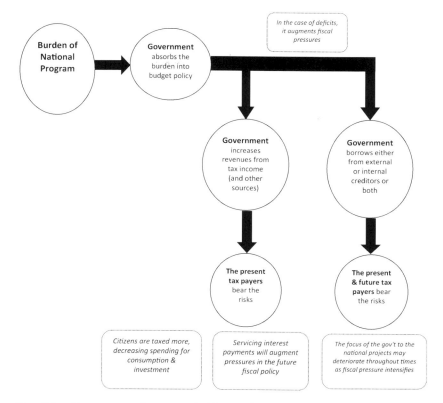

Fig. 3.1 Government finance and risk transfer management

investment. More often than not, reduced consumption and investment do not lead to increased employment and output, despite attempts by governments to increase aggregate demand through their spending. While the second alternative, borrowing, may not lead to reduced private sector consumption and investment immediately, it will lead to such pressures on the economy in the medium and long term (Swastika, 2016). External debt service drains resources out of the economy and domestic borrowing exacerbates income inequality considering that only the rich, the well-off and the financial institutions that manage their money hold a lion's share of government debt. Both external and domestic debt impose large burden on the future generation who will have to pay the taxes needed to service the debt created by the government that manages risks on behalf of the present generation. Transferring and/or shifting risks of financing fiscal deficits create myriad of problems for the present and future generations as lays the foundation for crises. As Reinhart and Rogoff (2009) demonstrate, all financial crises throughout history have been debt crises, that is, transferring/shifting risks of financial transactions through the workings of interest-rate mechanism renders the economy unstable susceptible to recurrent crises.

The alternative to interest-rate driven debt financing is risk sharing. In contracts based on risk sharing property rights claims are created only if the parties to the contract share the risk of the transaction according to their ability to assume the risk (Askari et al., 2014) and the burdens as well as the rewards of the undertaking. Risks and associated costs, if they materialize, and the rewards when they are accrued, stay within the domain of the contract and shared among the participants. They are not transferred/shifted to third parties. In theory, risk sharing divides the burden of economic and financial risks among economic agents. This is an important attribute of risk sharing. All participants to a risk-sharing contract have skin in the game (Taleb, 2012) and cannot transfer/shift risks of the contract to another party. In a risk sharing-based financial system, "private risk," or risk created by private actor's business decisions, remains private.

In such a system, private agents participate in financing public investment national projects. The system allows equal access for public to participate in planning, organization, and financing of these projects and the system ensures that the yield on the projects is distributed according to the level of risk born by each participant. Such a system needs a robust regulatory, supervisory mechanism in its oversight toolkit to ensure that participants in risk sharing contracts are protected. In a risk sharing financial system, there is close coordination between the real and financial sectors of the economy as financial resources directly finance real sector activities.

As depicted in Fig. 3.2, in a risk sharing system, the responsibility for financing developmental projects is proportionally shared by governments, private sector and households. Hence, the system encourages decentralization of financing decisions as they relate to developmental projects such as infrastructural investment programs.

To facilitate the degree of financial inclusion through extensive participation by citizens, macroeconomic policies have to play a somewhat

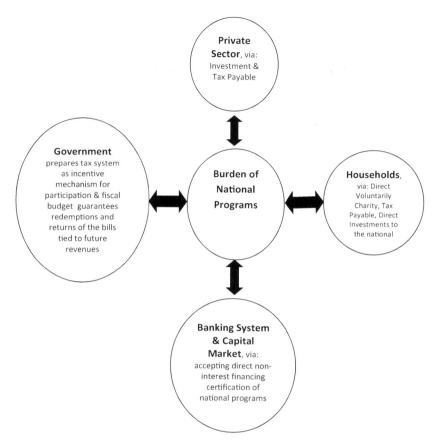

Fig. 3.2 Government finance and risk sharing management

unorthodox role of creating opportunities for this purpose. For example, the central bank could provide a special discount and rediscount window for commercial papers issued by the private sector in financing developmental projects and underwrite these securities, actions which renders these papers high-grade status. Fiscal policy too could provide special tax relief for business concerns that undertake public sector investment

28 P. SWASTIKA AND A. MIRAKHOR

projects, such as infrastructural development projects.[1] Questions may arise regarding the financial resources to finance these monetary and fiscal actions. In this context, it is worth recalling, as was pointed out in the Introduction to the book, establishing a risk-sharing system by eliminating the interest-rate mechanism, saves all the costs of operations of the massive edifice of the legal, legislative, administrative enforcement system needed to render debt contracts possible. Savings that thus accrue provides the resources to allow proactive monetary and fiscal policies responsive to the needs of real sector of the economy and the true risk manager of the society in its role relating to "*the stewardship of society's assets*".[2] In this context, the experience of German economy as it implemented risk sharing policies holds valuable lessons.

GERMAN ECONOMIC POLICIES: 1933–1935

An example of a successful economic policy based on risk sharing is implementation of such policy in Germany 1933–1935. The policy had led to a rapid recovery of the economy and eclipsed the performance of other European economies[3] during the Great Depression Era. In this policy, the Central Bank, "*Die Reichsbank*," established strong connection between the financial and the real productive sectors of the economy. The Bank operated under the monetary policy rule that allowed the money supply to grow in tandem with increase in production. Schacht[4] the President of the Central Bank at that time, wrote in his memoir: "*... I was able to break new ground. I abandoned the central banks' so-called classic discount policy. I embarked on a program of productivity expansion not dependent on savings (that is, on a restriction of capital expenditure) but on the actual*

---

[1] For studies of such proactive fiscal and monetary policies in support of risk-sharing financing of developmental projects and their impact on economic growth, see, Othman et al. (2017).

[2] Shiller (2011, pp. 7–9).

[3] The prominent economist John Maynard Keynes hailed the economic policies of Germany in the early 1930's in the preface to the German edition of his book "*The General Theory of Interest, Money, and Unemployment*" (1936) as "*contemporary method of resolving current problems of economy*".

[4] Hjalmar Horace Greeley Schacht (also known as "the Wizard") was the president of the Reichsbank for two terms (November 12, 1923–March 7, 1931) and (March 17, 1933–January 20, 1939). He was also the Minister of Economy from August 1934 to November 1937.

creation of wealth. I rejected the trading methods which traditional British economic theories had bequeathed " (Schacht, 1956, p. 471).

The above statement pinpoints the fundamental reform of monetary policy was to tie money circulation to production, in this case was the job creation programs. There was a public concessus among the German people that credit expansion was not an option because it would either jeopardize their asset and consumption due to financial burden from servicing interest rate, or force to hyperinflation situation—a condition where all Germans forefended. They feared that budget deficit, coupled with expansionary monetary policy, the 1923–1924 hyperinflation period could reoccur and further suppress their economic wellbeing. Therefore, the policy was to design commercial money-flow channels so that money circulated in support productive expansion.

The alternative macroeconomic policy in Germany in the early 1930s broke the risk transfer/shifting tradition. This policy smoothed money circulation, liquidated hoarded money asset, redirected these resources to real sector activities, promoted production, and, more importantly, enabled all agents of the economy to engage in promoting national economic recovery and development agenda of work creation. To spread the risk of fiscal budget, German policymakers deployed instruments, such as work-creation bills and tax-remission certificates, to induce participation of the private sector (businesses and households) in financing public infrastructure projects that created employment and provided jobs. These included: toll roads, residential houses, agriculture, railways, automobile industries, and other infrastructure projects. Work-creation bills thence became the instruments that mobilized and directed idle savings to financing public projects.

These commercial bills of exchange mobilized idle money resources, unemployed workforce, and excessive plants capacity to induce increase in employment, output and income needed to spur recovery from the depth of depression. Instruments issued thus were "*synchronized with the growth of* " (Schacht, 1967, p. 115). To make these instruments even more attractive, they were made discountable at banks and re-discountable at the *Reichsbank*. The process created what became known as "*Vorfinanzierung*," that is "Pre-financing" of projects from the idle finance capital of businesses and saving deposits of banks.

While the Government had committed itself to redeem these instruments, i.e., tax certificates and work-creation bills, the redemption was

30   P. SWASTIKA AND A. MIRAKHOR

Table 3.1 Allocation for jobs creation bills redemption

Budget 1934–35: 917 million marks
Budget 1935–36: 700 million marks
Budget 1937–38: 750 million marks
Budget 1938–39: 715 million marks

Source Baerwald (1934, p. 624)

optional. Moreover, the redemption mechanism was directly linked to the future budgetary receipts so that the annual conversion payments could not exceed government revenues of that period. Table 3.1 presented figures that show the annual budget allocation for redemption of these bills as follows:

Importantly, such characteristic distinguished the yield of these papers from the interest rate and made these financial securities instruments of risk sharing and effective means of financial inclusion as well as means of mobilizing idle savings to increased production, employment and income. During 1933–1935, inflation rate subsided and prices were stable leading to improved living standards after years of poverty and low consumption (Silverman, 1998, pp. 42–43). As well, conditions for production and business expansion improved. People regained their confidence to increase investment and production without fear of expropriation (Bel, 2006). As a result, trade revived (Poole, 1939), and "*national production rose 102% during 1932–1937, and the national income doubled*" (Shirer, 1962, p. 229). This substantial improvement was reflected in the labor market where new jobs were created. Unemployment reduced from 6 million in 1933 to 2.7 million in 1934, and 2.5 million in 1935.[5]

Germany challenged the prevailing methodology that wealth was created through "transfer of income," and innovated the idea that "creating income" through increased employment and output was the only method of achieving recovery and growth. The government changed the nature of national policy to orient its priority toward securing the interest of people by providing every citizen with a job (Schacht, 1967, pp. 113–116). Schacht subscribed to the sharing of risk-and-reward theory that emphasized the need for real productive effort and risk taking to underpin raising income. He stated, "*How to make money – this question and its attendant problems engage more of man's thoughts and efforts than almost*

[5] StatistischeBeilagezumReichsarbeitsblatt, 1928–1939.

3 RISK SHARING ECONOMY: A FRAMEWORK   31

anything else. The correct answer to the question is "through work and saving... (but) Making money always bound up with risks. He who seeks profits must be able to bear losses" (Schacht, 1967, pp. 8, 11).

The implication of such a fundamental shift in policy, in John Maynard Keynes' view, deserved praise. He asserted that the German way of managing the economy was *"a contemporary approach to our current problems.*[6]*"* Kenyon E. Poole, a Harvard economist, argued in his book **"German Financial Policies 1932–1939"** (1939) that *"The achievement of Germany in transforming herself from a financially and physically prostrate nation into a first-class world power in the brief space of five years has been looked upon by many observers as a 'miracle'... However, there is no mystery in the accomplishment... considering the all-encompassing revolution in tax, spending, and price policies under the Hitler regime. Even if they do not succeed in 'priming the pump' (i.e. increasing the volume of private investment), they form a necessary interlude until entrepreneurial initiative does revive."* A more recent analysis by Turgeon (Turgeon, 1997, pp. 1–2) suggested that Germany had implemented *"the neutralization of monetary policy,"* which technically meant pacifying interest rates in the economic system.[7]

In his report to National Resources Planning Board, Lewis L. Lorwin, a prominent American economist, wrote: *"A complete analysis and appraisal of German planning in all its phases are not intended here. The scope of this Report is determined by the fact that there is a widespread feeling that, whatever our attitude toward Nazi philosophy, its economic procedures may carry a lesson for democratic countries" (Lorwin, 1940, p. 3).*

---

[6] (The preface of The General Theory of Money, Interest, and Unemployment, German edition, Keynes, 1936).

[7] *"One of the features of Hitler's economy that also shows up in the General Theory is the neutralization of monetary policy... Hitler had a special aversion to interest as a form of income since he considered this return to capital to be 'parasitic.' Keynes in the General Theory has only a few references to monetary policy, and in one instance, he prescribed a lowering of interest rates in what we would later refer to as an overheated economy. He also prescribed the 'euthanasia of the rentier' or the eventual elimination of real interest in a mature capitalist economy. Subsequently... Sir Roy Harrods would also suggest the abandonment of interest as a category of income to pacify post-war socialists in Great Britain"* (Turgeon, 1997, pp. 1–2).

Epistemology of Risk Sharing in Islamic Finance

Abrahamic and non-Abrahamic religions as well as non-religious moralists thought consistently condemn the charging of interest. One reason why charging interest is viewed as breaching moral values and social justice, is that it creates income and wealth inequality and class conflict which undermines social solidarity and cohesion leading to social instability.[8] Moreover, interest rate-based contracts impinge on the rights of individuals and the society. For example, these contracts rely on collateral allowing lenders property rights control over borrowers' financial decisions. On national levels, interest-based contracts, impinge of the right of economies to economic self-determination.

Nevertheless, there is widespread belief that interest provides economic advantages and an incentive for the wealthy to extend credit to borrowers. It is believed that lending provides funding to spur production and consumption leading to profits. Therefore, it is legitimate for lenders to impose charges for loans paid out of business profits. Collateral, it is said, is justified since it only provides security for the lender against potential default of the borrower. Second, at the macro level, interest equilibrates money supply and demand efficiently.

However, economic history shows, at macro and micro level, interest rate-based system creates inefficiency in resource allocation, production, exchange and trade. It impedes financial resources from reaching their most productive uses, i.e., financing real sector activities. As Keynes argued, interest-rate mechanism creates frictions and imbalances in the circular flow if income such that saving-investment and aggregate supply and demand cannot equilibrate. The result is either unemployment and recession or over-heating of the economy and inflation, or even, at times, inflation and recession both. Moreover, since in an interest-based debt system credit history of individuals are indispensable to access to financial resources, many potential, productive entrepreneurs as well as many productive projects are excluded from the financial system.

In this context, Keynes (1931, 1936) argued that the interest rate mechanism creates a coordination problem between savers and investors

---

[8] Witness the recent events in the USA which demonstrate the breakdown in social cohesion and social solidarity as a result of years of erosion in social capital due to the rapid growth of income and wealth inequality and years of economic policies that impoverished labor and the middle class, and the growth of rentier economy.

and prevents savings from finding their most productive use in the real sector of the economy. A system in which this happens, he argued, creates two evils. First, it can never create full employment without government interference in the economy. Second, it skews income and wealth inequality for the rentier (see also Piketty, 2020). Further, Keynes asserted that the main cause of these two "evils" is the interest rate mechanism that is the "villain of the piece." In such a system, risks of a venture are transferred from creditors to debtors or shifted to unaware third parties. This happened in the 2007/2008 crisis as risks were shifted to taxpayers.

The above arguments undermine the strength of the efficiency reason given as a justification for the necessity of the interest-rate mechanism. Moreover, as it was explained in the Introduction, the efficiency argument is further weakened by the significant, but hidden, costs associated with the operations of an edifice of monitoring and enforcing "impossible" interest-based debt contracts. It has been shown that—to top all other inefficiencies—such a system is unstable and prone to repeated crises.

Compelling arguments have been made that the alternative to a system of interest-based debt finance, with all of its inefficiencies and injustices, is a risk-sharing financial system in which all participants have skin in the game; a system that avoids many ills of debt-finance system including its instability (Askari et al., 2014; Rafi, 2017, 2020). Risk sharing means that the risk of a venture is allocated to the participants based on the ability of each participant to assume the risk. In this system, the return is not fixed ex anti but based on the return to activities that risk-sharing has financed. The system works efficiently in an open and dynamic capital market environment where investors are offered financial instruments long-term that match participants' risk appetite. New entrepreneurs attract investors by proper disclosure of their enterprise's prospects promoting financial inclusion. Risk sharing, thus, obviates the need for debt-based instruments or money markets.

Risk sharing is the "salient feature" of Islamic finance (Kuala Lumpur Declaration, 2012). There are three ways of managing risk: transfer it, shift it, or share it. In the first case, risks of a venture are transferred from one party in the transaction to others. In the event of risk shifting, all the risk of the operations are shifted to third parties without their knowledge or consent. Risk sharing allocates the risk of the venture to all parties in a transaction according to each participant's ability to carry risk. Since Islam prohibits interest rate-based debt contracts, it means that it prohibits risk transfer or risk shifting. This is the reason Muslim jurists issued the 2012 Kuala Lumpur Declaration (*Fatwa*) that risk sharing is the essence of Islamic finance.

What is specific about Islamic finance is its emphasis on rules governing exchange transactions. In an exchange transaction, there is a mutual sharing of risk and reward between two or more parties immediately upon offer and acceptance. In sale, lease, partnerships and other trade-based contracts, all parties are required to assume the risks of transactions. The parties must disclose accurate information related to the dealings. An agreement between the parties establishes the legitimacy of any exchange deal. Thus, the parties should not sense duress when making an offer or agreeing on the terms and conditions of a contract.

Risks of a transaction are managed by transferring, shifting or sharing them. In the first case, risks are transferred to one of the parties to the transaction. For example, in the demand deposit transaction between the depositor and the bank, the risk of the funds deposited is transferred to the bank. In a bank-loan contract, the bank transfers the risk of the loan contract to the borrower. In the second case, the risks of a given contract or a transaction are shifted by the parties in the contract to a third party without its knowledge or consent. Islamic finance considers interest-based debt contracts as risk transfer. The interest rate charged adds a fixed percentage of the principal to a loan contract. The emphasis is on the ex ante flat rate, i.e., a stipulated percentage of the principal imposed even before the onset of the project for which the loan is required. The predetermined amount represents the lender's property rights claim on the borrower. For the borrower, interest rate becomes the cost of obtaining money while it is a premium for the lender. Thus, by charging an interest rate on lending, financial resources are transferred from the deficit units to the surplus units without a corresponding transfer of property rights or risk level to the lender. As the evolution of the financial sector over the past five decades reveals in an economic system where risk transfer dominates, the financial sector decouples from the real sector such that only a small fraction of financial resources is allocated to the productive sector as capital.

At a macro level, risk sharing offers a method where citizens participate directly in financing public sector projects, i.e., programs supporting infrastructure and social development projects that spur employment, income, and growth. Thus, citizens share responsibility with the government for ensuring progress and success of the programs, which alters the role of fiscal policy assumed in conventional system significantly. Using risk sharing to finance development expenditures eases pressure on fiscal policy. Governments no longer need to resort to debt-creating flows to finance their development budget. Debt servicing has been a source of serious instability in many developing and emerging market economies.

Turning to monetary policy, in the conventional system, monetary authorities have to rely on banks to transmit its measures to the private sector to induce portfolio adjustment. However, because in this system monetary authorities and the banking system have different objective functions, often the latter is reluctant to transmit monetary policy to the private sector. This phenomenon has been observed in many countries where monetary authorities implemented an accommodative policy of low (at times negative) interest rates, through expansion of money supply (quantitative easing) to stimulate investment. Under Islamic finance, the monetary authority (the central bank) can perform its mandates of economic growth and stability by using the rate of return to the real sector as the instrument of monetary policy, while maintaining a rigorous payment system. This way, monetary policy would influence the private sector's asset portfolio adjustments directly.

An Islamic economic system envisages the development of both human and economic as primary objectives. Human development refers to nonphysical achievement described by a state of contentment and happiness, including a peaceful and stable environment. Economic development relates to substantial progress associated with prosperity. The vision of this economic system is enshrined in institutions, such as social and economic justice, equality of opportunity, justice in exchange, and distributive justice (Askari et al., 2014, pp. 76–80). Prohibition of risk shifting and risk transfer is central in organizing strong market institutions, such as trust, transparency, and cooperation. Risk sharing requires that all participants in a given economic or financial venture have "skin in the game" in the form of equity. In other words, resources are allocated based on risk-reward relationship. Therefore, it is a system based on universal principles that ought to serve all people for the same common interest in prosperity regardless of apparent differences among them.

Muslim scholars agree the foundation of Islamic finance is Verse 275 of Chapter 2 of the Holy Quran (2:275). The Verse provides the organizing principle of the Islamic financial system. It contains four aspects: (i) the consequences of the risk transfer-based system; (ii) the characteristics of

36   P. SWASTIKA AND A. MIRAKHOR

the proponents of the risk transfer system; (iii) the negation of interest-based systems; and (iv) provision of guidance and incentive structure for implementing risk sharing.

The Quran (2:275) full text proclaims, "*Those who devour Riba (risk-transfer mechanism) will not stand except as stand one whom the Evil one by his touch hath driven to madness. That is because they 'Al-Bay' (risk-sharing) is like Riba (risk-transfer),' and Allah has allowed Al-Bay' and forbidden Riba. Those who after receiving direction from their Lord, desist, shall be pardoned for the past; their case is for Allah (to judge). However, whoever returns to Riba, such are the dwellers of the Fire - they will abide therein.*"

The first point: "*Those who devour Riba (risk-transfer) will not stand except as stand one whom the Evil one by his touch hath driven to madness*" (Quran, S2:275:1).

This part of the verse implies the inherent instability of risk transfer and risk shifting transactions.[9] The illustration is drawn from the verse, "*as stand one whom the Evil one by his touch hath driven to madness,*" is a metaphor to describe the constant cycles of instability and insecurity in the social, economic, and finally political situation.[10] A market dominating risk transfer practice turns fundamentally unstable where cycles of recession, boom, and crisis exist. In such systems, stability is a mere mirage because institutions and structures cannot coordinate economic plans of agents.[11] In such a system, the financial sector decouples gradually from the real sector through a process of financialization (Abdulkarim et al., 2020), as the financial sector grows to dominate all other economic sectors leading to recurrent episodes of instability. Economic stability needs third-party (peer groups and government) efforts to enforce rule compliance and coordination that are essential in organizing a robust

---

[9] These are the interpretation of the first part of the verse from an economic point of view. However, the foundation for such commentary is sourced from Ahmad al-Wāhidī (2008), Tafsir Al-Mizan by Allamah Muhammad Hussein Tabatabai.

[10] "*The commonly understood meaning is the one given by Ibn 'Atiyyah, because when the word -standing- is used, one generally understands it to mean managing some affairs; and there is no association to show that it refers to the rising from grave*" (At-Tabataba'i, 1981).

[11] Allah swt used the word "*yatakhabbat*" to refer the quality or state of those persons who commit to *Al-Riba*. Some translator of Al-Qur'an refers this word to "madness" (as translated above). Nevertheless, the word is derived from the word "*Al-Khabt*" which means "disorganized (or disoriented) movement" (At-Tabataba'i, 1981).

and resilient market to withstand crises and large swings in economic activity.[12]

From a micro perspective, risk-transfer exacerbates future uncertainty for both borrowers and lenders. For borrowers, uncertainty arises from the mismatch between the obligation to service the loan and the expected future financial flows necessary to the service of the loan. According to Keynes, interest rates aggravate the problem of coordination between saving and investment.[13] For the lenders, financial certainty only occurs after due diligence of the credibility of the borrowers and their ability to maintain the payment structure. In other words, lenders always prepare for the worst—loss of their financial resources due to default, costs of litigation and recovery from the non-compliant borrowers. While customarily collateral is used to secure the lenders' interest, it does not necessarily minimize the uncertainty of losses. Should borrowers fail to meet their obligations, restructuring the payment schedule may have only a minimal effect on smoothening contract performance, especially if lenders still imposed interest rate on the new structure.

The second part of the Verse relates to the response of the proponents of the interest rate mechanism. This group is identifiable from their response quoted in the Quran, "*That is because they say: Al-Bay' (risk-sharing) is like Al-Riba (risk-transfer contract)*" (2:275).

The part suggests two important implications. First relates to the question of who made the statement? Some commentators of the Quran refer it to nonbelievers, others to the confused group of individuals in the first part of the verse. The Verse may refer to anyone—believers and nonbelievers—who is unable to distinguish between good and evil; those who have lost the cognitive ability to recognize the consequences of their decisions and actions. Second, by claiming "*likeness,*" these people mean that they do not see any difference between *Al-Bay'* (risk-sharing contract) is like *Riba* (risk transfer and risk shifting contract) because of apparent

---

[12] These "large swings" would not exist in an Islamic economic and financial system.

[13] Keynes explained the negative relationship between interest rate, investment, and savings. He wrote: "*The attractiveness of investment depends on the prospective income which the entrepreneur anticipates from current investment relatively to the rate of interest which he has to pay to be able to finance its production… It follows that an increase in the rate of interest tends to make the rate of investment to decline relatively to the rate of saving…*" (Keynes, 2013, p. 139).

resemblance between the two systems or even the possibility of the arithmetic equivalence in the outcome of the two types contracts. They argue that *Al-Bay'* (mechanism of risk sharing) and *Al-Riba* (mechanism of risk-transfer and risk-shifting) intermediate between financial surplus holders and deficit units; both are means of mobilization and distribution of financial assets.[14]

Risk sharing, risk shifting, or risk transfer are tools of risk management.[15] However, risk sharing differs significantly from risk shifting or risk transfer. The objective of risk sharing is to pool risks and to allocate it among participants according to their capacity for risk bearing (Mirakhor, 2011). The common examples of risk sharing instruments are equity stock, sharecropping, and partnership contracts. Risk transfer and risk shifting, on the other hand, create a setting or incentive for a party to move the risk to counterparties or third parties with or without their knowledge or consent. An example of latter is all bail-out programs encountered during the aftermath of the 2007/2008 financial crisis that shifted their costs to the present and future generations of taxpayers.

Commentators of the Quran are often perplexed by this part of the verse by posing an intriguing question: *why do people assert that Al-Bay' (risk sharing) is like that of Al-Riba (risk-transfer and risk-shifting), and not the other way around*? Some views, such as the *Tafsir-al-Jalalayn* (2007, p. 51), explain the phenomenon from a linguistic perspective. The interpretation suggests the claimants are aware of the function as the distributional channel for finance and the objective of both systems which is to earn a profit. The feature also develops the argument that criticizes the higher status of *Al-Bay'* over *Al-Riba* received its legality from the Creator's Commandment. The focal point of comparing *Al-Bay'* to *Riba*, and not the other way around, is the planned, structured actions of the claimants for rejecting *Al-Bay.'* Another reading is the implied characteristic of the applicants who treat both systems alike. Such a feature is indeed noticeable in the present time where Muslim bankers, financial

---

[14] Some commentators, such as Tanwir al-Miqbas min Tafsir Ibn 'Abbas, explained the form of *Al-Bay'* on the deferred sales which allow for the price to increase carries the similar end with that of *Al-Riba* which the lender stipulates the predetermined interest rate in the beginning of transactions (Ibn Abbas, A Maududi, n.d.).

[15] To avoid confusion, risk here is defined as potential bad outcomes. Hence, economic risk is potential bad outcomes of an investment due to macroeconomic instability. Financial risk is bad outcomes from financial transactions.

experts, and policymakers see only a minor difference between financial services based on *Al-Bay'* and on *Al-Riba*.

The verse continues with the third part that makes it a cornerstone rule governing the Islamic financial system. This section asserts *Al-Bay'* as the only alternative method for economic mobilization and renounces the use of *Al-Riba*. Allah SWT says: "*And Allah has allowed Al-Bay' and forbidden Al-Riba*" (Quran S2:275:3).

The sentence is a clear-cut source of legal rulings and a cornerstone of jurisprudence in Islamic finance.[16] Ordaining *Al-Bay'* (risk sharing) and prohibiting *Al-Riba* (risk transfer and risk shifting) are Divine rules with which those who believe must comply faithfully, believing that full compliance with this rule is better for themselves and the humanity. Religious experts reinforced this understanding of the spirit of Islamic finance. For example, in 2012, a group of Muslim scholars and jurists issued the "*Kuala Lumpur Declaration*," a strong call to financial institutions and Muslim governments to adopt risk sharing. *Al-Bay'* as instrument of risk sharing fosters social cohesion, increases cooperation and better coordination as everyone is bonded to one another in a particular financial relation either as partners (as in a *musharaka*[17] contract), or capital contributors and entrepreneurs (as in a *modaraba*[18] contract). Risk sharing contracts set clear rules of rights and obligations and of rewards and liabilities, for those who have "skin in the game," workers, financiers, and entrepreneurs. They have an inherent incentive structure that promotes honesty and trustworthiness while reducing the costs of contract enforcement and litigation. On the other hand, risk transfer encourages concentrating risk on the shoulders of entrepreneurs/labor while the capital owner assumes minimal risk.

It has been argued (Iqbal & Mirakhor, 2011, pp. 64–65) that *Riba* breaches Islam's rules governing property rights which does not permit instantaneous property rights claim without commensurate work and labor. Interest on money loaned constitutes such a claim and, therefore, it has no standing as a legal mechanism to claim rights of possession on

---

[16] It is acknowledged that this part of verse is not the sole legislation forbidding *Al-Riba*. The scholars of The Qur'an identified that this verse came later than verse 130 of this chapter.

[17] *Musharaka*, or *al-Sharika*, means partnership contract.

[18] *Modaraba*, means silent partnership.

40 P. SWASTIKA AND A. MIRAKHOR

borrower's property.[19] At the closing years of the first millennia (C. E.), Al-Ghazali provided an explanation for the prohibition of *Riba* which was used also by medieval scholastic scholars. Al-Ghazali wrote: "*Al-Riba is prohibited because it prevents people from undertaking real economic activities. This is because when a person having money can earn more money by interest, either in a spot or deferred transactions, it becomes easy for him to earn more money by interest without bothering himself to take pains in real economic activities. This leads to hampering the real interests of humanity because the interests of humanity cannot be safeguarded without real trade skills, industry, and construction*" (*Al-Ghazali, Iḥyā'ᵡ Ulūm al-Dīn, as cited by Qal'awi [1998] in Usmani, 2010*).

Muhammad Hussein Tabatabai elaborates further in *Tafsir Al-Mizan* that social disharmony, conflicts and eventual disintegration are consequences of operations of risk transfer/shifting systems. He wrote: "*As for Al-Riba, it caused the treasures of the earth to be concentrated in few select houses and the wealth to be hoarded by the rentiers. The money gave them power over other less fortunate human beings. It was the real cause of the world wars. It divided humanity into two opposing groups: the wealthy who enjoy all the blessings of life, and the poor who find it difficult to meet their barest needs. The grouping has already appeared... It is threatening humanity with downfall and the world with destruction.*"

The last sermon of the Prophet ﷺ during his last pilgrimage covered, inter alia, the economic and social costs arising from the operation of Al-Riba *(interest-rate based debt contracts)*: "*O People, just as you regard this month, this day, this city as sacred, so regard the life and property of every Muslim as a sacred trust. Return the goods entrusted to you to their rightful owners. Hurt no one so no one may hurt you. Remember that you will indeed meet your Lord and that He will indeed reckon your deeds, Allah SWT has forbidden you to take Riba; therefore, all interest obligations shall henceforth be waived. Your capital, however, is yours to keep. You will neither inflict nor suffer any inequity. Allah SWT has judged there shall be no Al-Riba and*

---

[19] The rules of Islam strictly hold sacred the property of rights to human, thus regulate the avenue for which the claim must adhere the following condition; First is that the claim of property is generated only from two origins: (a) income distribution, i.e. a combination of individual's labour, skill, and natural resources, and (b) income redistribution, i.e., the remittance from the more able to the less able segment. Second, that *riba* (in banking term, lending) cannot generate rewards ["*Nor expect, in giving, any increase (for thyself)!*" (Al-Qur'an verse 6, Chapter 74)]. Therefore, the rules of Islam dismiss legitimacy in charging interest rate on top of a loan contract.

3 RISK SHARING ECONOMY: A FRAMEWORK 41

that all interest due to Abbas Ibn Abd al Muttalib (the Prophet's uncle) shall henceforth be waived" (The Last Sermon of Prophet Muhammad ▓).

It is instructive to note references to words "inflicting" and "inequity" in this passage in light of recent findings from studies that refer to the trillions of dollars in costs "inflicted" and the resulting injustices and inequities created by the operations of a risk transfer/shifting financial system. In 2013, the Government Accountability Office of the United States estimated that the financial crisis' toll on economic output might be as much as $13 trillion; the wealth lost by US homeowners amounted to $9.1 billion (GAO Report, January 2013). Another 2013 study by Federal Reserve staff found the costs of the crisis could be $14 trillion higher than the previous estimate if the loss of economic output and the wealth of citizens (Atkinson et al., 2013) are included. These studies, however, did not cover the "additional and potential costs" related to unemployment (the loss of income), significant psychological and social costs that are immeasurable yet affect future economic output significantly. These studies confirm empirically the economic and human costs of operations of an interest rate based system against which the Qur'an and the prophetic tradition warn.

The fourth part of the verse provides the all-important incentive in form of Creator's forgiveness for those who repent from charging interest in the past *"… Those who after receiving command from their Lord, desist [entering into interest based contracts], shall be pardoned for the past; their case is for Allah (to judge) …"* Quran (S2:275: 4).

In a saying reported from the Messenger, all participants in contracts that transfer/shift risks of a transaction are warned: *"Allah SWT cursed whoever consumes Riba, whoever pays Riba, the two who are witnesses to it, and the scribe who records it"* (Sahih Muslim). The Messenger applied the Creator's command in case of a dispute between two tribes of *Thaqif* and *Mughirahin* which the former claimed interest payment in addition to the principal loaned to the latter. Once this dispute was reported to the Messenger by the Governor of Mecca, he ordered the tribe of *Thaqif* to forego the interest payment and receive only the principal.

Eliminating the interest-rate mechanism is the cornerstone of an equitable financial system. To be equitable, the system creates equal access to financial resources for all segments of the society and demands fairness in public access to economic opportunities according to their skills and expertise. The needs of the economically-least-able segment of the society are covered by the system of distribution and redistribution. On the contrary, financial systems that rely on the interest-rate mechanism, pass financial risks of a transaction to borrowers and third parties but benefit the financial surplus holder, thus creating and widening the gap between income and wealth disparity and creating social division (Piketty, 2020). The system also discriminates against innovative entrepreneurs without credit history and against capital-intensive businesses, such as renewable energy, green technology, and transport, as the premium for borrowing is significantly larger than that in typical businesses of manufacturing, oil mining and refinery, and even banking, insurance, and financial industries (adverse selection). Islamic finance guarantees that no surplus beyond the principal shall be paid to the lender. Because of this tenet, some have been naively criticizing Islamic finance principles as being the cause of the economic backwardness of the Ottoman Empire and the Middle East (Zaman, 2011).

The main argument of critics centers on the idea that economic growth needs capital accumulation. The rules of Islamic economic and finance, such as prohibiting interest rate, the Islamic inheritance system and "trust" institutions, such as waqf, reduce the ability of an individual to accumulate wealth that would lead to financial capital buildup. Critics also assert the inefficiency of the trust (*waqf*) system, the system of *zakat*, and the failure of partnership arrangements in facilitating economic development and growth. They consider accumulation and concentration of wealth as a major factor for growth and prosperity while neglecting other institutions that contribute to economic prosperity and social solidarity, such as trust, rule compliance, social cohesion and solidarity. Some Western scholars, such as Joseph Stiglitz, suggest that capital accumulation has failed in promoting an equitable mobilization of capital and providing solutions for today's socio-economic problems (Stiglitz, 1989).

Islamic financial system focuses on establishing an efficient means of answering the fundamental questions of "what to produce"? "how to produce"? and "for whom to produce"? These questions relate to allocation of resources, production, exchange, distribution and redistribution in any system. The system is built on two organizing principles of endorsement of risk-sharing and prohibition of risk-transfer system. It is asserted that this system is more efficient than the present-day dominant risk-transfer system based on the historical accounts that document the positive impact of risk-sharing arrangements on economic growth and social development.

The following chapters will review some of these developments in Europe which linked partnership financing structures with socio-economic development, in the *Renaissance* during the Middle Ages and the Medici Bank (de Roover, 1963), as well as in Venetia as a maritime trading center (de Lara, 2005; Lara, 2006; Norwich, 1977; Puga & Trefler, 2012), or the beautification of the city of Paris, or the building of railroads by *crédit mobilier* (Cameron, 1953; Newmarch, 1858; Walsh, 1856). These historical developments contradict firmly the arguments of the critics of Islamic finance, for example, that risk sharing is unproven in modern, complex societies, and ex ante interest rates are an indispensable as benchmarking and referencing tool. The criticisms also seem unfamiliar with the knowledge of Islamic law and jurisprudence, and the vision of Islam for economy and finance. It discounts rules governing economic behavior that promote better and more efficient resource allocation and distribution to achieve growth, welfare, and prosperity for all members of the society.

The incentive structure in the fourth segment of the Verse relates to forgiveness of the past lapses that are subject to the judgment of the Creator alone. It raises the hope that prolonged and repetitive crises can be eliminated if humans avoided transactions based on risk-shifting and risk-transfer. It offers an incentive to embrace risk-sharing system as the organizing framework for financial and economic affairs. It can be a prescription to end the endless cycles of booms and busts that impose enormous economic costs and distress to humanity.

Finally, the fifth part of the Verse refers to the disincentive to discourage participation in interest rate-based transactions, "…*but whoever returns (to Al-Riba), such are the dwellers of the Fire -they will abide therein*" (Quran 2:275).

So far, the practice of Islamic finance has yet to emerge as a complete risk-sharing system as prescribed by the Qur'an. The current applications of Islamic finance in Muslim countries still do not meet the fundamental principles of that system. The dominant practice is to eliminate the word "interest" in the financial contract and replace it with a benchmark rate. This, however, does not eliminate the adverse impact of interest rate on the pricing mechanism of economic and financial products and services. A recent study by Alaabed (2016) confirms the observation that majority of Islamic banks in Malaysia, Saudi Arabia, Bangladesh, Indonesia, and Kuwait, engage in risk-shifting with various degrees of intensity. It also appears that practitioners treat Islamic finance as an asset class in the conventional financial system (Alam, 2008; Iqbal, 1997; Mirakhor, 2011). The reason for such condition is the absence of political will, commitment and resolve to design and implement risk-sharing system at the national level (Mirakhor, 2011). As such, there is a lack of clear direction for Islamic financial institutions. This situation is responsible for the ongoing misconceptions about Islamic finance.

The ideal Islamic financial system requires risk-sharing embedded in macroeconomic policies. The government, as the mandated risk manager for the society as a whole, must ensure the method applied is efficient in minimizing society's risk and producing prosperity for its people. That said, the manner of managing economic risk must be able to address current problems of unemployment and income inequality and provide welfare to all segments of the population, especially the economically least able. Under the risk-sharing framework, fiscal policy aims at providing a healthy circulation of economic resources and smoothing consumption. Fiscal barriers that impede private sector's participation, such as complex tax structures, are repealed and replaced by simpler and more equitable structure that rewards participation and promotes social solidarity. Monetary policy must ensure there is no coordination problem between savings and investments such that the financial sector could provide for the productive sector's need for financial resources. The Verse of the Quran 2:275 can be understood as envisioning a stable and robust economy by promoting allocation of financial resources to most efficient uses in the productive sector of the economy. The existence of the interest-rate mechanism, as argued by Keynes, creates coordination problem by causing frictions and obstructions to the smooth flow of financial resources from the surplus to deficit units and to their most productive uses.

In an economic system based on Islamic rules, justice is served when financial resources find their optimal use and money circulates freely as means of exchange. Demand of fairness would be fulfilled by providing equal access to the financial resource available. This system creates financial and non-financial incentives which will eliminate speculative and unproductive activities.

References

Abdulkarim, F. M., Mirakhor, A., & Hamid, B. A. (2020). *Financialization of the economy and income inequality in selected OIC and OECD countries: The role of institutional factors*. De Gruyter.

Alaabed, A. (2016). *Risk shifting and Islamic Banking*. INCEIF.

Alam, M. S. (2008). Islamic finance: An alternative to the conventional financial system. *Korea Review of International Studies*.

Askari, H., Iqbal, Z., & Mirakhor, A. (2014). *Introduction to Islamic economics: Theory and application*. Willey (Asia) Pte. Ltd.

At-Tabataba'i, M. H. (1981). *Tafsir Al-Mizan*. World Organization for Islamic Services.

Atkinson, T., Luttrell, D., & Rosenblum, H. (2013). Assessing the costs and consequences of the 2007–09 financial crisis and its aftermath. *Economic Letter, 8*(7).

Baerwald, F. (1934). How Germany reduced unemployment. *The American Economic Review, 24*(4), 617–630.

Bel, G. (2006). Against the mainstream: Nazi privatization in 1930s Germany. *SSRN Electronic Journal*. https://doi.org/10.2139/ssrn.895247.

Cameron, R. E. (1953). The credit mobilier and the economic development of Europe. *The Journal of Political Economy, LX, 1*(6), 461–488.

Çizakça, M. (2011). *Islamic capitalism and finance: Origins, evolution and the future*. Edward Elgar Publishing Ltd.

Çizakça, M. (2014). *Islam and the challenges of western capitalism*. Edward Elgar Publishing Ltd.

de Lara, Y. G. (2005). *The secret of venetian success: The role of the state in financial market* (No. 1). Alicante.

de Lara, Y. G. (2006). The secret of venetian success: Public-order yet reputation-based institutions. In *XIV International Economic History Congress*. Helsinki.

de Roover, R. (1963). *The rise and decline of the Medici Bank, 1297–1494*. Harvard University Press.

Iqbal, Z. (1997). Islamic financial systems. *Finance & Development*, June ed.

Keynes, J. M. (1931). *Essays in persuasion*. Macmillan & Co. Ltd.

Keynes, J. M. (1936). *The general theory of employment, interest, and money*. Palgrave Macmillan.

Lorwin, L. L. (1940). *Public works and employment planning in Germany 1933–1939*. Washington, DC: National Resources Planning Board.

Mirakhor, A. (2011). Risk sharing and public policy. In *The 5th international Islamic capital market forum*.

Newmarch, W. (1858). On the recent history of the credit mobilier. *Journal of the Statistical Society of London, 21*(4), 444–453.

Norwich, J. J. (1977). *Venice: The rise to empire*. Allen Lane.

Othman, A., Sari, N. M., Alhabshi, S. O., & Mirakhor, A. (2017). *Islamic finance, risk sharing, and macroeconomic policies in book macroeconomic policy and islamic finance in Malaysia*. Springer. https://doi.org/10.1057/978-1-137-53159-9_4.

Oxfam. (2016). *An economy for the 1%: How privilege and power in the economy drive extreme inequality and how this can be stopped* (No. 210).

Piketty, T. (2020). *Capital and ideology*. Belknap Press.

Poole, K. (1939). *German financial policies, 1932–1939*. Cambridge, MA: Harvard University Press.

Puga, D., & Trefler, D. (2012). *International trade and institutional change: Medieval venice's response to globalization* (No. 9076).

Reinhart, C., & Rogoff, K. (2009). *This time is different*. Princeton University Press.

Schacht, H. (1956). *Confessions of "The Old Wizard"*. Cambridge, MA: The Riberside Press.

Schacht, H. (1967). *The magic of money*. London: Oldbourne Book Co. LTD.

Silverman, D. P. (1998). *Hitler's economy: Nazi work creation programs, 1933–1936*. Cambridge, MA: Harvard University Press.

Shiller, R. J. (2011). *Finance and the good society*. Princeton University Press.

Shirer, W. L. (1962). The rise and fall of the third reich: A history of Nazi Germany. *The American Historical Review, 68*(1), 126. https://doi.org/10.2307/1847219.

Stiglitz, J. E. (1989). Financial markets and development. *Oxford Review of Economic Policy, 5*(4), 55–68. https://doi.org/10.1093/oxrep/5.4.55.

Swastika, P. (2016). The relative contribution of debt to Indonesian growth: A case study using Wavelet analysis. *Journal Ekonomi dan Bisnis Islam, 2*(1), 1–17.

Taleb, N. N. (2012). *Antifragile: Things that gain from disorder*. Random House.

Turgeon, L. (1997). *Bastard Keynesianism: The evolution of economic thinking and policy making since World War II*. Praeger.

Walsh, R. H. (1856). *Notes on the Société Générale de Crédit Mobilier*.

Zaman, A. (2011). Review article: Timur Kuran, the long divergence: How Islamic law held back the Middle East. *Islamic Studies, 49*(2) (2010), 277–286.

CHAPTER 4

Historical Review of Risk Sharing Instruments

This chapter presents a broad historical and economic review of the evolution of risk sharing instruments. The chapter comprises two sections: section "Risk Sharing Application in Conventional Literatures" examines the historical use of risk sharing in commercial transactions and businesses. It further offers information about the various risk sharing financial tools that merchants and traders used in risky transactions from the Middle Ages up to the nineteenth century. Section "Evolution of Public Finance Instrument: Public Finance Instruments in the European Land" covers the evolution of public finance in the European and Islamic region under the Ottoman Empire.

RISK SHARING APPLICATION IN CONVENTIONAL LITERATURES

Risk sharing was not an innovation of modern economics and finance. In fact, markets would not have developed and sustained without participants embracing risk sharing. The design and principles underpinning risk sharing fortified commitment and trust among market actors to honor exchange obligations, an act of sanctifying the rights of property. Economies flourished when people shared the risk of productive activities for the purpose of income generation. However, at some point in

© The Author(s), under exclusive license to Springer Nature
Switzerland AG 2021
P. Swastika and A. Mirakhor, *Applying Risk-Sharing Finance for Economic Development*, Political Economy of Islam,
https://doi.org/10.1007/978-3-030-82642-0_4

47

their history, motivated by greed, humans learned they could potentially gain more if they transferred or shifted risks of transactions to others through the use of interest-rate mechanism. This myopic and self-serving development was not costless as it breached the sense of community and brotherhood, individual freedom and sovereignty over their economic life, principles that had undergirded social solidarity and helped the survival of collectivities.

As risk transfer/shifting gained momentum beginning in the fourteenth and fifteenth centuries, commitment to morality and ethics in human relations weakened leading to erosion of social capital, especially trust (Ng et al., 2015). Erosion in social capital led to insecurities, social tensions, and instability. Concurrently, accumulation of wealth by rentiers created massive income inequality (Piketty, 2014) and class conflicts are further weakening social solidarity and cohesion. Witness the social, political, economic, and health crises ongoing across the world which in large measure is due to the injustices of the dominant economic and financial system the world over.

As Reinhart and Rogoff (2009) showed, historically, all financial crises including the one in 2007/2008 were in essence debt crises; an outcome of operations of risk transfer/risk shifting dominated financial system. Such systems are prone to developing debt bubbles that more often than not burst causing economic crises. In each bubble episode financial sector activities per se expands, new instruments of risk transfer/shifting are innovated but financial inclusion is seldom strengthened. For example, in the buildup to the 2007/2008 crisis, under the guise of "democratizing finance," highly opaque, complex instruments were introduced that, in hindsight proved to hurt the people who were to be the beneficiary of these innovations, poor and middle class homeowners (Mian & Sufi, 2014). Financial inclusion remained limited but "financialization"—the process of rapid growth of the financial sector far outstripping the expansion in the real sector—spread rapidly to the point of near decoupling the two observed currently.

Economic history has recorded the evolution of partnerships in Europe since the medieval period. However, this form of business organization became most popular. It was no coincidence that these arrangements more popular in the *Renaissance* era (beginning of the fourteenth century until the seventeenth century). The legacy of this era is celebrated not only for the rapid development of art and culture but also for the expansion of commerce, markets, and institutions. Historians have labeled this period "*The Late Medieval Commercial Revolution*" (Greif, 1994; Lopez, 1976). During this period, financial institutions ventured with artisans, painters, wool and silk manufacturers to pursue commercial activities, with artisans as the active agents. Risks and rewards were shared. This arrangement allowed partners to engage directly in commercial transactions without exposing their entire wealth, thus reducing potential risks.

From fourteenth to nineteenth centuries, financing structures based on partnerships expanded rapidly from the Mediterranean Sea to Northern Europe. Their influence on the developing society and the world of commerce was immense, particularly in Italy. Historians documented diverse applications of regional partnership patterns. They appeared as ventures, such as *commenda*,[1] *societas maris*,[2] joint-stock banks, like the *Medici Banking House*. The House of *Medici*, established in Florence, employed variety of partnership forms. It is reported that it was the first financial institution in Europe to use the accounting method known as double-entry bookkeeping as well as limited liability structure (*società in accomandita*). De Roover, in "*The Rise and Decline of the Medici*" (1963), documented details of joint venture contracts between the *Medici* and co-partner artisans, and how the Bank had used partnership structures

---

[1] *Commenda* was the dominant financing structure based on partnerships. It had flourished in the thirteenth century throughout the Western Mediterranean. It influenced the economic development of the Italian coastal cities, such as Venice, Genoa, Pisa, expanding to the Spanish and French coastal cities. Based on the merchants' liability arrangement, two general types of *Commenda* were mostly applied in the region: (i) "*Accomendatio*" the standard unilateral *Commenda*, and the "*Societas Maris*" (standard bilateral *Commenda*) (de Lara, in Mokyr, pp. 481–483).

[2] In *Societas Maris*, the partners contributed to the business capital. If *Commenda* reflected dormant and active partnerships, in *Societas Maris* the partners took part in the liability altogether. The merchant contributed one-third of capital; the other partners contributed to the remaining two thirds. By this arrangement, the merchant received one-half of the profit (*cum ista societas nominatur*). In principle, *Societas Maris* was like the standard *Commenda* mechanism, with two extensions on the capital contribution (the risk) and loss/reward portion. Hence, the difference between *Societas Maris* and *Commenda* lied solely in the risk sharing (Weber & Kaelber, 2003).

50   P. SWASTIKA AND A. MIRAKHOR

to extend its branch network to other cities.[3] Moving slightly northward, historians have recorded the contribution of the *commenda* contract as a powerful financing instrument had promoted trade and expeditions in Venice. Thanks to this mode of financing, Venice was transformed from an agrarian lagoon to the largest commercial Centre in Italy where money rapidly circulated through trade.

In its first adoption in Europe, *commenda*[4] was unlike the existing modes of financing commonly practiced in the European Community (Puga & Trefler, 2012). The funding system that emerged in mid-thirteenth century quickly replaced the infamous sea loans that finance risky, remote trading. Long-distance sea voyages were risky because of unpredictable **weather**, long sail time and the deadly threat of piracy. In addition, private bankers imposed excessive interest rates on these loans. Lopez described sea trading *"like the land trade (that) called for closer collaboration than that of a straight loan"* (Lopez, 1976, p. 76).

By *"closer collaboration"* Lopez meant the bond between investors and sailing merchants to mitigate risks of trade. The risky nature of the voyage called for substantial capitalization before sailing.[5] *Commenda* backed this significant amount upfront by inviting investors to participate with any size of investment as "shares." In return, the investors trusted that the sailing merchants would endeavor to return the vessel safely profit. It

---

[3] According to de Roover (1963, p. 78), in 1457, Cosimo di Medici announced that eleven entities (manufacturer and branch) the house was the majority shareowner, of which all were organized and managed under the partnerships. They were: (1) the bank in Florence, (2) two wool shops in Florence, (3) one silk shop in Florence, (4) the Medici's house in Rome, Venice, Milan, Geneva, Avignon, Bruges, and London.

[4] Translated as "recommendation" or *colleganza/collegantia* that is "colleagueship."

[5] The ships were loaded with goods and resources and needed to be in the best condition to sail with adequate tools to provide safety and security throughout the long journey (up to 5 months). The type of investment which was predominant during the early stage of Commercial Revolution was high risks investment. Lopez marked: *"High risks and high profits.... were instrumental in forming the first accumulations of capital and lifting a few intelligent and fortunate merchants above the general mediocrity of early medieval trades. Three successive Commenda agreements of 1156–1158, whereby a Genoese investor trebled his initial investment of slightly more than 200 pounds, and the travelling party earned almost 150 pounds as his share of the profits, are a characteristic example of good fortune. Later, competition forced down the average profits, but greater security and the widening of the market enabled careful managers to increase their assets more steadily than ever before"* (Lopez, 1976, pp. 97–97).

was also customary that sailing merchants were transparent in their financial reporting. Upon their return, they declared profit and loss within 30 days and distributed the profit among the investors commensurate with each share. At times, profits amounted to over 100% (Puga & Trefler, 2012).[6] Hence, *commenda* was a partnership-based financing structure that converted trade uncertainties into manageable shared risks.

Several variations of *commenda* developed during the Middle Ages in the Europe: *rogadia, societas, fraterna, compagnia, column*, and *cerati* (Çizakça, 1996; Lopez, 1976).

Rogadia: merchants combined their efforts and used each other's capital goods without compensation. They then transported and traded the goods in other markets and declared the profit or loss from the venture to the original owners of the goods upon their return.

Societas: a contract where partners pooled their capital and labour and shared both profits and risks. This partnership assumed unlimited liability for the debt of others.

Fraterna: a partnership contract where the capital goods were jointly managed by two or more brothers (of the same family) and invested in trade.

Compagnia: a partnership contract that included less-close relatives—cousins and sons-in-law—in the joint administration of goods in restricted dealings for a limited amount of money in a brief period. Regardless the restrictions, all partners of compagnia bore unlimited business liability.

Column: partnerships between the captain, sailors, merchants and those travelling on the ship; all impacted working capital according to their contribution.

Cerati: an investment contract that divided the estimated working capital for a ship into small-sized shares among most investors. Italian maritime centers (Genoa and Venetia), as well as England and the Hanseatic region, appreciated this partnership (Çizakça, 1996; Lopez, 1976).

According to economic historians, such inclusive risk sharing financial methods had enabled the development and growth of these cities. Market institutions from foreign cultures widely influenced this movement. Their intensive interaction with more advanced economies was

---

[6] The ships were loaded with goods and resources and needed to be in the best condition to sail with adequate tools to provide safety and security throughout the long journey (up to 5 months).

inevitable, thanks to international trade. Through foreign transactions, merchants exchanged with local trader's basic market principles, rules and norms of trade and methods of financial arrangements. Borrowing institutions from more advanced economies were necessary for less-advanced nations because effective market institutions reduced transaction costs, thus accelerating economic growth. The most important of these was *commenda*. Historians have established that *commenda* originated from "*modaraba*" (Çizakça, 1996; Udovitch, 1962).

In *modaraba*, the capital owner and the entrepreneur together carried the business risks and shared the profits (losses). Unlike transactions based on risk shifting/transfer, entrepreneurs divided profits based on an agreed-upon formula. Financial losses were restricted to the capital owner, while the entrepreneur endured the loss of efforts, time, and possibly reputation. Europeans adopted and integrated the principle of risk sharing through *commenda* and gave it legal status. Although emanating from a foreign culture and tradition (i.e., Islam), the community accepted and embraced the principles of risk sharing and established legal instruments to ensure effective enforcement of the provisions of risk sharing contracts (Çizakça, 2006).

Commenda spread rapidly throughout Europe. Islamic by nature and therefore non-usurious, the Church had sanctioned it. During the eleventh–thirteenth centuries, European merchants legalized the "*Law Merchant of Europe*" (Lex-Mercatoria) that originated from the commercial texts in the Muslim regions. Khalilieh (2006) argued "the Maritime Laws of Rhodes were based on *Al-Mudawwana al-Kubra* by Sahnun ibn Sa'id al Tanukhi (d. 854)." In the eleventh century, Sicily in Southern Italy—Muslim territories—redrafted the law. The Court of the Crusader Kingdom of Jerusalem authored "*The Maritime Laws of Oleron*." Eleanor of Aquitaine brought one part of it into Europe, and her son Richard the Lionheart brought in the rest. The Oleron script was identical to those in Muslim countries during the ninth–tenth centuries.

"*The Consulato del Mare*," written in Barcelona, originated from the Muslim Middle-Eastern texts of the eighth–the ninth centuries. In the thirteenth century, King Alphonso had the law translated during his reign. When the European community embraced these merchant's laws; they essentially adopted the Arab traders' principles of risk sharing as an accepted universal value and norm promoted by the Arab traders. Through *commenda*, Venice was transformed from an agrarian to a global maritime center.

Evidently, the growing economic pie was distributed mainly among the middle-income group. This event created an inevitable political tension between the rising middle class and the wealthy elites who felt threatened. Consequently, between the late thirteenth century and the early fourteenth century, Venice experienced a revolt of the noble and wealthy families, known as the "*serrata*" (the lockout). Acemoglu and Robinson (2012) classified "*serrata*" into two types: (i) political *serrata*, and (ii) economic *serrata*. The motive behind *serrata* was clear. The wealthy nobles wanted to recuperate their power and permanent position in the City Council and the economy. In the political arena, they wanted to control the public and to create a separate segment for the non-elite groups. Through the political *serrata*, the nobles used the legal rules to ban the practice of *commenda*, so that new or non-noble merchants had no access to financing. In economic affairs, they wanted to stop the rising of middle-income merchants and to reclaim their share in the economic pie as before the eleventh century. Through the City Council, this elite group also gave more control to the Government to influence the private sector's initiatives to investment or participate in long-distance trade by imposing high taxes on trade. This development, called "*The Oligarchs Triumphant*" (Norwich, 1977, Chapter 13) finally led to the decline of the Venetian economy.

Commenda was the forerunner of joint-stock companies. The first of joint-stock companies established in England in the mid-sixteenth century were the Russian, Levant Companies[7] and the "East India Company" (Harris, 2000, p. 24; 2009; Poitras, 2016, pp. 138–185). Scott (1912) added the "Adventurers to Guinea Company" (1553) to the list.[8] Later, the "Royal African Company" and the "Hudson's Bay Company" followed the earlier enlisted firms (Baskin & Miranti, 1997).

---

[7] The Russia Company was also known as the Muscovy Company and the Levant Company was known also as the Turkey Company. These companies served long-distance markets to the outside of Europe and to other continents, for instance the Muscovy traded with Russian markets while the Levant traded with Turkey and the Eastern Mediterranean (Harris, 2000, p. 43).

[8] According to Scott (1912), the Adventurers Company was unfortunately short-lived due to crisis. Investors withdrew his/her capital from the firm after the Wars and economic crisis affected the firm's performance significantly. A different fare experienced by the Russia Company, as they were monopolizing the European wax market hence increased its capital. The company, then, issued the fractional shares and the share was understood to be "a part" in the business.

Italians who settled in the English lands introduced the natives to this financial innovation. Mainly from Florence and Venice, these Italians instructed the English merchants how to undertake foreign trade service using *commenda* contracts (Scott, 1912). Thus, these companies collected capital from private investors to conduct far-distance trade with isolated areas, such as Russia, Africa, and Asia. At the end of the project, stockholders received their profits based on their share ownership. Though *commenda* allowed capital to be collected on an ad hoc basis (per voyage), the English joint-stock companies accepted capital partnerships more widely, ranging from six-month to permanent and perpetual capital. The East India Company, known as the oldest joint-stock company, had established permanent capital in 1657. On the other hand, the *Verenigde Oost-Indische Compagnie* (V.O.C. or *Dutch United East India Company*) had locked their investors in long-term commitments half a century earlier. This factor determined the success of V.O.C. in monopolizing the sea trade with Asia.

The perpetual capital was an important attribute of capitalization and business sustainability as it reduced transaction costs. It transformed a short-term *commenda* into long-term partnership entities that secured stability for the organization to continue venturing and innovating. Çizakça (1996) explained how and why capital structure evolved from an ad hoc basis to a more complex perpetual capitalization. Referring to the case of *Verenigde Oost-Indische Compagnie*, Çizakça observed, three forces drove the short-term capital company to adopt the permanent capital structure: (i) competition that propelled smaller firms to merge into one large corporation. The V.O.C. was an example of successful mergers that reduced transaction costs arising from stiff competition; (ii) the expansion of the investor base, most of whom did not know the managers that conducted business, created a shift in the investment attitude from personal to the company relations; and (iii) the evolution and innovation of legal products and instruments which allowed third party (government) regulation and supervision of capital-formation contracts covering the spectrum of time performance of capital formation, from short- and medium-term to a long term and perpetuity.

Such government intervention gradually converted joint-stock companies from ones focused on private interests to become oriented toward national interests. As in the V.O.C. case, the government's order to invest significant amounts of its capital for building estates at home and fortification along the coasts of West and South Africa set a condition for the "*Staaten Generaal*" to change its the focus on private interests to center on national interests. The outcome immediately affected shareholders' status from "*partners in a ten-year venture*" to "*shareholders of a corporationthat had assumed a perpetual existence*" (Çizakça, 1996, p. 46).

The late seventeenth and eighteenth centuries were the heydays of the joint-stock system. By early 1687, the number of joint-stock companies mushroomed. In 1694, the system had become the national "engine" for the growing maritime enterprise and colonization (Scott, 1912, p. 441). Scott also discovered data that disclosed the increasing amount of capitalization of joint-stock ventures. They grew from £10,000 (or about 0.013% of GDP) in 1553 to about £50 million (around 13% of GDP) by 1720.[9] This data points to the high productivity periods of the joint-stock system. Therefore, from the Commons to Royal investors, everyone was tempted to invest in this profitable market.[10] The outcome evoked an unprecedented social phenomenon—a close interaction between immigrants and natives. The London alley markets became the hub for important commercial and social events. This enthusiasm was well-covered in the main financial publications of the time.[11]

Until the *South SeaBubble* crisis in 1720, the joint-stock system served as an efficient tool for channeling capital to risky investments few had wanted to commit to before. The system was acknowledged for its distributive feature—channeling savings to the otherwise excluded untapped segment and breaking the aristocratic domination of the heavily regulated companies and guilds. The system also provided capital for skillful artisans, merchants, and sailors.

The system's advantages were manifold. For investors, the joint-stock system provided alternative investment opportunities with limited liability

---

[9] Scott further added: "... *It must be noted that an organization had come into being, which, by 1720, possessed the control of funds at least as great as the whole estimated amount of the trading wealth of the country*" (Scott, 1912, p. 440).

[10] Scott (1912, Vol. 1, p. 446) summarized the yield of the joint stock firms over the years. Between 1568 and 1573, *unsuccessful years*, yielded a division of no less than 106%. Between 1608 and 1615 yielded total divisions of 339%, *that is an average of over 42% per annum*. Between 1611 and 1612 (period of 2 years), 90% yield was *divided on each occasion*. For more discussion on risks, profits, and losses of joint-stock companies, see William Robert Scott, *the Constitution and Finance of English, Scottish, and Irish Joint-Stock Companies to 1720* (Vol. I, Chap. XXII, pp. 446–448).

[11] See Harris (2000), and Natasha Glaisyer, *The Culture of Commerce in England, 1660–1720* (2006/2008, pp. 102–108).

without daily hands-on risk management operation. Also, the liquid shares of joint-stock companies were conveniently tradable without significant costs or legal sanctions. The system further created a deeper and more liquid stock market, especially during the sixteenth century. The shares were traded with "*a considerable degree of freedom*" (Scott, 1912, p. 443). In other words, by freely trading the stock, investors benefitted from lower transaction costs.[12] As for the firms, joint stocks enabled them to become financially more flexible, efficient in agency costs, and more sustainable than the regulated businesses or guilds.[13] These benefits reflected in the real example of the joint-stock system, such as the East India Company.

The financial collapse of 1720 had exhibited the fraudulent financial practices of the risk transfer system. Scott (1912) asserted that the swap between the loan of the English Government and the South Sea Company stocks was the gate for speculators to bid for the odds that may have caused the crisis. Speculators deceived stockholders for they knew the conversion would contribute nothing but losses to the company. The swap between government loan and company equity increased the company's stock prices by leveraging debt and interest commitments and not by increase in fundamental value of the company. The scheme included £31 million, of which "*one annuity, totaling £15 million, matured in 72–87 years and paid 7% annually; the other, totaling £1.5 million, matured in 22 years and paid 9% annually. Besides the annuities, there was outstanding £16.5 million in a redeemable loan that was less burdensome because its interest rates periodically adjusted to declining market levels*" (Baskin & Miranti, 1997, p. 108). If all debt were converted, "the value" of the company would have been summed up to £42.75 million (Scott, 1912).

---

[12] Transaction costs consist of not only the costs of coordination and managing information of the business activity so that measurement of value would be made easy, but also the cost of contract enforcement and commitments "*across time and space*" (North, 1991, p. 6).

[13] Baskin and Miranti noted several benefits of the joint stock form (1997, pp. 60–62). They are: "*(1)* **financial flexibility** due to the tradable shares, *(2)* **quick restructuring** in comparison with alternative business forms, *(3)* **permissible by the Church as equity was not usury**, *(4)* **reduction in information costs**, *(5)* **lower agency costs**. For more discussion on the key drivers of the successful joint-stock system between 1553 and 1720, see also Scott (1912, Vol. 1, pp. 442–444). However, opposing views contend the inefficiency of the joint stock system; see for instance Ron Harris (2000), *Industrializing English Law: Entrepreneurship and Business Organization, 1720–1844*, p. 85.

Consensus among economic historians refers to the aftermath of the 1720 financial crisis as a "*disaster*" and "*financial setback*" for causing a 50-year delay in the Industrial Revolution (Easterly & Stiglitz, 2000).[14]

As to bookkeeping, the conversion from equity stocks to debt indeed increased the company's value, with assets instantaneously concentrating on the receivables account. Further, the company's share price augmented by the undertaking increased the market value and turned into a benefit for shareholders and the company. For the State, the deal had eased the balance sheet for two reasons. First, the government gained as much as £7.5 million from the contract fee paid by South Sea; and second, a reduction of the debt servicing costs was expected since, presumably, handling one creditor was easier than several. However, concentration on the receivables made the liability account worrisome; it was considered a personal risk until the obligations were cashed out. Despite these risks, South Sea was eager to seal the contract with the government, lured by speculations of instant profits, continued increase in stock price, and the net cash profit from debt conversion.[15] Such short-term minded business decision eventually shifted the risk of the whole economy.[16]

Despite the market panic, the stock exchange performed on a decent scale. The deep secondary market had helped the primary market to recover, notwithstanding the occurrence of several smaller crises. The surviving companies were enterprises with real undertakings. The secondary market supported them with substantial contributions, thus

---

[14] The South Sea bubble crisis created a setback in the financial system, to the capital market. People began to distrust financial institutions and it started government intervention into financial market through The Bubble Act of 1720 that limited the use of joint stock corporations until the nineteenth century (Neal & Schubert, 1985).

[15] "*According to Archibald Hutcheson, with South Sea stock at 125, the net cash profit would have been £480,000, with the stock at 150 it would have been £3,707,500*" (Scott, 1912, Vol. I, p. 410).

[16] It is important to note that during the South Sea financial fiasco in England; there were also concurrent crises in the French and Dutch markets. Although the details of the events perhaps varied from one market to another, the sequence and the root of problems is, however, broadly the same. That is, the risk-transfer State economic policy that permitted risk-shifting behaviour (including leveraging with junk assets) by rent seekers and speculators. For a thorough discussion on the South Sea and Mississippi bubbles, see Scott (1912), *The Constitution and Finance of English, Scottish, and Irish Joint-Stock Companies to 1720*, Vol. I; and for a discussion on the "speculators" role in the crisis, see Neal and Schubert (1985), *The First Rational Bubbles: A New Look at the Mississippi and South Sea Schemes*.

stabilizing the effect of the market crash and sustaining their capitalization. For these businesses, the stock market was the only source of capital for projects and commercial expansion in the Far East, Africa, and the Americas. Notably, these companies also restored investors' confidence through their business accountability.

Evidence concerning the economy of England during the period indicates that small joint-stock companies flourished and remained productive despite the adverse impact of the crisis. Indeed, the crisis had weakened the capital market, especially since confidence plunged in the then so-called "*Moneyed Companies.*" The joint-stock financing remained the favorite method for firms to capitalize their business. Payne suggested, "*The essential simplicity of so many of the productive processes, characterized as they were by a growth pattern involving simply the multiplication of units, rather than by radical re-organization, allowed continued direction by the single entrepreneur or by the small group of enterprises far bigger than had once thought workable. These factors enabled manufacturing and trading firms to grow without recourse to the joint-stock form*" (Payne in Mathias & Postan, 1978, Vol. III, p. 195).

The joint-stock system had a distinct advantage over legal commission structures in financing costly public projects, such as transportations. It was said, by the advocates of the joint-stock system, that the original undertakers were flexible to transfer projects' ownership and entitlement to the new investors, and invite more investors into the projects without worrying about legal status (Harris, 2000, p. 92). This approach clearly showed one of the competitive advantages of the joint-stock companies over other business forms for mobilizing capital effectively for large projects even when the capital market seemed bearish. The total capital amount covered the issued shares from wide-range of investors based on their ability to put skin in the projects.

Moreover, the joint-stock system needed a robust secondary market otherwise, the system would be vulnerable to liquidity crises and not survive. As documented, the state restricted, or acted against, developing the joint-stock system by delimiting the power of private joint-stock enterprises and increasing state control. They also promulgated parliamentary acts and statutes to ban the so-called unauthorized transfer of ownership and support to the statutory Navigation Commission. These legal efforts were futile as investors and entrepreneurs evaded the legal authorities and kept the joint-stock system functioning privately. Henceforth, the passing of acts and statutes did not alter the standard but merely tightened the foothold of risk sharing finance throughout the eighteenth century and the first half of the nineteenth century. It became a major driving force for the recovery.[17]

Some have argued that the joint-stock system changed the way of business conduct. From the *commenda* to joint-stock enterprises, artisans, merchants, sailors, and others who possessed the required skills focused their expertise on production and innovation, not worrying about securing finance for their projects on their own. They concentrated on making strategic business decisions, conducting business for the best possible outcome and sustaining the firm. As for financing, the shareholders carried the funding responsibility and enjoyed power and control over the company. This capital arrangement converted the risk of total loss to one limited to the value of the shares. Thus, the system was more equitable than the alternative, particularly for "risk-averse" middle-class investors and skillful artisans who could not afford the statutory (or chartered) claim from the state.[18] Investors received their share of the profit proportional to their willingness to assume business risk taking and accountability. This share paper was termed "equity."

The early nineteenth century marked a new phase for the joint-stock structure to integrate with the European banking sector. In 1822, Belgium founded the first European joint-stock investment banking company, "*Algemeene Nederlandsche Maatschappijter Begunstiging van de Volksvlijt*" (known as *SociétéGénérale*). Also, in 1822, a mass movement in Britain forced a reform in the financial market against the monopoly of the Bank of England. In 1826, the Parliament finally issued "*The London Act of 1826*"—The Banking Co-partnership Act. The Act abolished the domination of Bank of England and leveled the playing field for

---

[17] "*Starting from a long-term average of not more than 3 percent in the seventeenth and early eighteenth centuries, the rate of capital formation began to rise in the middle decades of the eighteenth century; by the end of the century it had reached a 'sustained average of more than 5 percent' and 'may have somewhat exceeded 6 percent-most of the shift being attributable to the last quarter'*" (Feinstein in Mathias & Postan, 1978, Vol. VII, Part).

[18] It is acknowledged there is a litigation issue comparing unincorporated companies with incorporated joint-stock companies that in the case of disputes amongst the partner–partner or partner–manager, the earlier type could not be sued in the legal courts as they are unchartered. Nonetheless, we consider that although such conditions might have increased investor's litigation risks, it did not substantially deteriorate the substantial contribution of the joint-stock system to economic development, of England, parsimonious to the historical facts historians have recorded.

60 P. SWASTIKA AND A. MIRAKHOR

smaller financial firms. The legislation established pathways for merchants and middle-class investors and formed middle-sized financial institutions patterned after the joint-stock firms. These companies were allowed to participate in financing city projects, such as building canals and turnpike roads. Merchants and investors also favored joint-stock banks for their stability over the conventional model of private banking.[19] Similar mass movements also occurred across Europe one decade later, exemplified by the European transport system as in the case of the French "*Crédit Mobilier.*"

Established in November 1852, "*Crédit Mobilier*" (officially, "*Société Générale du Crédit Mobilier*" or "*Société Générale*") began as a joint-stock company, "*en commandité*" (limited liability). Its initial capital amounted to 2,400,000 *livres*, distributed in shares of 20 *livres* each (Newmarch, 1858). *The Banking House of Fould's* was the majority owner of the shares (60%)—Achille Fould was the Finance Minister of the Second Empire. One hundred shareholders, politically prominent and socially important figures in the Second Empire, except the Rothschilds, secured the remaining 40% (Cameron, 1953). The exclusion of Rothschild was intentional, mainly because Napoleon III, the new ruler, wanted to strengthen his government control over public projects (particularly the French railroad system) and to be less financially dependent on the Rothschild and their allies (Cameron & Bovykin, 1991, p. 8; Smith, 2006, pp. 82–83).

From its beginning, the entity had been promoting their economic values and wisdom which contrasted with the common practice. As stated in the published Company Statutes, "*The Société Générale will perform the office of an intermediarybetween Capitalists and Industry. It will put an end to the difficult conditions commonly exacted for definitive investments in Industry*" (Newmarch, 1858). The critical mission of the company was to set a new course for the financial institution, vested in the role of "*intermediary*" (or intermediaries), in departure from the traditional activity of lending money. Pursuing this mission, *Crédit Mobilier* became

---

[19] The York City and County Banking Company Prospectus declared: "*The security (of joint stock form) not being dependent on the wealth, ability, or conduct of particular individuals* (original version would have been in italics), *is not affected as in private partnerships, by the death or retirements of elder partners, who commonly constitute the stabilityand experience of their respective concerns*" (Newton, 2007).

the first "entrepreneurial bank"[20] in the Continent (Drucker, 1998). Soon after, other financial institutions in different States had emulated this banking concept.[21]

The founders of *Crédit Mobilier*, Emile, and Isaac Pereira introduced "new banking techniques" in finance. The principal role of *Crédit Mobilier* was to fund everything merchants and industrialists wanted—particularly movable properties and transport projects—thereby the term "*mobilier*". They also financed immovable properties, such as land and house mortgages. Then, the general role of the *Crédit Mobilier* followed the principle: "*It employs its money... in buying up shares in other Companies, managing the affairs of this latter, or taking part in their management... and then reselling them for whatever they may bring in the market*" (Walsh, 1856). The Annual Report of April 1860 interpreted the principle of the company's policy: "*Our company has always considered as a principle of its high commercial morality never to open a subscription, nor recommend a firm, without first having a large part of interest in it and its administrators having become associated with it*"[22] (Paulet, 1999, p. 31). To that end, the company had placed its representatives in every

[20] The description "entrepreneurial bank" means a financial institution which extends the capital from depositors and shareholders primly for projects and commerce activities generating economic development.

[21] Darmstädter Bank (or, *Bank für Handel und Industrie*), for instance, was modelled after the *créditmobilier*. The Industrial Bank of Japan (founded in 1900) and "*other financial institutions in India*" also emulated the model of *créditmobilier* (de Aghion, 1999). R. Cameron and Bovykin (1991) also enlisted Stockholm Enskilda Bank while explaining that *Crédit Mobilier of America* was a fraud institution which pirated the name of the institution. They quoted a passage taken from *The Economist* to show the great influence of the bank to the economies of other lands, briefly after its inception in November 1852: "*... the manner in which the French capitalists are extending their relations is most remarkable... they have established Crédit Mobilier in Madrid and Turin, are about to do the same in Lisbon, and are trying to do the same at St. Petersburg and Constantinople... they have established a large bank at Darmstadt, and will not rest until they get one at Constantinople;...*" (*The Economist*, July 12, 1856 in Cameron & Bovykin, 1991).

[22] The original texte states, "*Notre société a toujours considéré comme un principe de haute moralité commerciale de ne jamais ouvrir une souscription, de ne jamais recommander une enterprise sans s'y intéresser même dans une forte proportion, et ses administrateurs se sont fait un devoir de s'y associer*" (Paulet, 1999, p. 162). (Our enterprise has always considered it a principle of high commercial morality never to open an underwriting, never to recommend an enterprise without much interest in it, and its directors have made it their duty to associate.).

business management they financed through partnership. The investment account recorded these relationships, and the mechanism accounted for the larger part of the total investments.[23] This condition formed the ideal "ecosystem" that provided direct investments in productive firms and financed public-sector projects (mainly railways and transport) to create employment and spur growth.

The vast array of operations required a significant amount of capital, for which three sources were available: (i) the nominal capital of the institutions raised through stocks; (ii) the current account deposits; (iii) debenture papers "Bonds," issued for raising more capital to finance projects outside the country. There was a distinct feature of the bills with bonds as the company described and promised the security of the redemption as they aspired: *"The superiority of the Constitution of the Society General consists of the scheme which it includes for the emission of Obligations at Long Term in such a manner that the repayment of the obligations will proceed, pari passu, with the redemption of the shares and bonds which the Society will hold in its portfolio"* (Newmarch, 1858).

Walsh (1856) explained the contour of payments attached to the value of the underlying investments: *"There are two kinds of the company's "bonds:" the first, issued for a short time, must correspond with the company's various temporary investment. The second, issued with unknown dates of payment and reimbursed by redemption, will correspond with the investments of like nature which we (Crédit Mobilier) shall have made either in rentes or shares and debentures of manufacturing companies"* (Quoted from the Crédit Mobilier Report, April 23, 1856, in Walsh).

The mechanism enabled the company to establish a more efficient risk management system, compared to the conventional practice, since liabilities of securities matured parallel to the collected receivables of its investment. By its nature, it resembled venture capital in its present form. It also allowed the bank to offer capital owners an option based on investment preference, thus increasing the perceived benefits on yield and providing financial stability.

---

[23] Conventionally, according to Paulet (1999), such policy was deemed to be risky as major part of the bank's portfolio was unsecured by collateral. Further, she documented that *"... (the CréditMobilier) never asked for guarantees from the affiliated companies"* (Paulet, 1999, p. 33). Based on the corporate statement and the absence of collateral/guarantees for its financing activities, therefore it is safe to conclude that most (if not all) the corporate strategy was to be active in equity-financing, and not extending funds in lending mechanism.

It is also important to understand the nature of the Company's portfolio. Studies described the investment portfolio of *Crédit Mobilier* as "full of high-risk ventures" (Cameron, 1953; de Aghion, 1999; Newmarch, 1858; Walsh, 1856). Conventional financial theory considered projects "high risk" (railways, canals and city planning) for being capital-intensive investments that required substantial cash and public guarantees. As an investment bank, *Crédit Mobilier* was involved in the stock-jobbing activities; that is, buying up shares of companies (promising, but with low price), took part in their management, then sold the shares at higher prices (Walsh, 1856, p. 352). Further, these investments did not yield immediate returns, they were long-dated and had inadequate collateral for recovery. From this viewpoint, *Crédit Mobilier* regarded these projects risky indeed.

Crédit Mobilier undertook the establishment of the Western, Southern, and Eastern Railway Companies, the Austrian Railway, the Ardennes and Pyrenean Lines, the Swiss Railways, and the Spanish Railways. It also undertook the beautification project of the city of Paris. Moreover, it formed the General Omnibus Association and Maritime Association by purchasing 60 vessels, sailors, and steamers, and reorganized the Gas Companies in Paris (including the Central Gas Company), and their notable acquisition of several saltworks in Southern France. Since these projects were all long-term public projects, investors could not gain returns immediately. Guided by institutional objectives, the company collected no collateral or financial guarantees from project partners, hence, increasing the risk of losing investment. To counter the risk, the bank assigned its members to represent it on the boards of the ventured enterprises or projects, thus, securing the bank's interests and, subsequently, reducing the perceived risks.

Another risk factor was the ability of *Crédit Mobilier* to manage their extensive array of businesses. Management policy specified the capacity (skills, expertise, and human resources) of *Crédit Mobilier* to oversee and supervise properly the ventured businesses, particularly those where the bank was an active partner. Under this perspective, mainstream lending mechanisms were less risky as they did not require direct involvement in the borrower's business. The unorthodox organization and policies of *Crédit Mobilier* exposed it to management risk, then unknown in the traditional business of private bankers.

Alongside these factors, it was not uncommon to find criticism about *Crédit Mobilier*'s financial inclusion policy for extending its services

64   P. SWASTIKA AND A. MIRAKHOR

to those "*least favored by fortune*" (Walsh, 1856, p. 354). From the viewpoint of conventional corporate finance, these risk factors—significant investment capital, the absence of collateral, longer-term return on investment, and limitations on management capacity—contributed to the increased portfolio risk of *Crédit Mobilier*. Nevertheless, investors continuously flocked to invest and take part in the company's expansion until its competitors, the Rothschilds, forced it out of the market in 1867.

Trust is an invaluable capital for financial institutions. Since its establishment, *Crédit Mobilier* was known to value philanthropy and equality in capital distribution. The company sought preservation and promotion of human welfare as well as the provision of work for the unemployed. Considering that *Crédit Mobilier was*, beyond doubt, a private profit-seeking business, it is debatable whether it was inspired by the Saint-Simonian principle.[24] The corporate business of "microfinance" was only a small part of the company's overall endeavors. The attribute of the assigned representatives in the management of the ventured businesses was essential to corroborate the success or failure of the enterprise.

Unfortunately, in 1856, *Crédit Mobilier* was hit by two public scandals that cast serious doubts on their integrity and business performance and severely tarnished their image. Worse yet, the loss of public trust exacerbated the Bank's troubled services. The first incident was the personal bankruptcy one of the Bank's directors, M. Place. He was arrested for fraud by creating false personal financial reports to secure personal loans to cover his speculative investments to falsify the fact that his debt obligations were beyond his capability to service them. He was forced to declare

---

[24] Many scholars associate Saint-Simonians teachings with socialism and collectivism. Such perception is what debatable. But it is a fact that Saint-Simonians vision of unity and coordinated economy had inspired Émile and Isaac Pereira to establish the Society General based on principles that emphasized predominantly on entrepreneurships and efficient resource allocation (Eckalbar, 1979). Saint-Simonians also known to criticize division of labor based on consumption activity, i.e., producer and consumer, and proposed with one based on productive activity, that is the idle class that "owns and does not work", and the labour class that "works without possessing". They also denounced the *laissez-faire* and competition concepts, since such elements would result in socio-economic problems and crises. As such, Saint-Simonians proposed for an organized and administrated economy that "*(1) the instruments should be distributed in accordance with the needs of each locality and each industry, (2) they should be distributed in line with each individual capacity in order to be implemented in the hands of the most able*, and *(3) production is so organizes that one should never be afraid of suffering from any starvation or congestion*" (Zouache & Boureille, 2009).

bankruptcy and sued for conveying deceitful information to lenders. Since Mr. Price was one of the directors of the Bank, the case significantly hurt the Company's reputation. The second incident, later in the same year, was the prosecution of M. Goupy, one of *Crédit Mobilier* shareholders, on the charge of misreporting to shareholders the fact that the company had incurred a loss. These cases had a negative impact on the morale of the directors and eventually precipitated the decline in the company's performance henceforth.

The hallmark of the phenomenal launch of *Crédit Mobilier* and its success resulted from the shift in the method of its financial intermediation and its approach to banking operations. The company was a triumph over the old-fashioned banking hegemony dominated by a few private banks, such as the *Rothschilds* and *La Haute Banque*. For some, Louis-Napoleon's support to *Crédit Mobilier* was celebrated as a new era of innovation in public finance and banking, particularly with the low-middle class engaging more directly in public projects. Public participation was an important feature of the company's corporate structure as the shareholders across Europe funded the infrastructure projects. It was a significant contrast to the old regime whose activity was restricted and dictated by a few wealthy individuals.

The business model of *Crédit Mobilier* had demonstrated the potential of the joint-stock system and was indeed a source of inspiration for participation-based financial innovation. As a matter of fact, its closest rival, the Rothschilds, were forced to emulate *Credit Mobilier*'s business strategy in order to secure advancements in the Austrian railway's project. Promoting the business strategy of joint venture in banking was an important legacy of *Crédit Mobilier*. Walsh explained, "*Much is said about companies supplanting the private trader, but the truth is, the kinds of business in which such succeed are most of those which, if there were no companies, would not be carried on at all, or else be conducted in a most unsatisfactory manner… as a general rule, it may be laid down that without the combination of the pecuniary means of many individuals, works of that description would rarely be attempted; and hence they afford an appropriate field for public companies*" (Walsh, 1856, pp. 353–354).

In the twentieth century, the first venture capital company was established in the United States. Based on similar business philosophy as *Crédit Mobilier*—an intermediary between capitalist and industry— venture capital was an approach to reach potential groups of artisans and entrepreneurs whom banks charged high lending rates. Thus, risky investments dominated the portfolio of venture capitalist because this method of financing required no collateral. There are at least two differences between the venture capital model and that of *Crédit Mobilier*: (i) the status of the company's investors; and (ii) the degree of involvement in the business operations. Unlike *Crédit Mobilier* that sold shares to retail investors to raise capital, the main source of venture capital financing is wealthy individuals or a combination of funding companies, such as pension funds and investment banks as well as educational institutions with large endowments as is the case with many USA universities using their endowment funds to purchase company shares (Çizakça, 2011, p. 252).

Another differences between venture capitalists model and that of *Crédit Mobilier* is the degree of involvement in managing companies they finance. The main goal of a venture capitalist is to prepare companies to register in the capital market. In return for the provision of financing, the venture capitalists obtain part of shares of the company based on mutual consent of the parties. *Crédit Mobilier*, on the other hand, remained involved in the day-to-day business operations of the companies in which it invested and sometimes took on the projects fully under its own management. In sum, both venture capitalist and *Crédit Mobilier* models allowed capital owners and entrepreneurs to share business losses and profits and establish a close link between capital, entrepreneurial, and productive activities. At this point, it is worth mentioning that both venture capitalist and *Crédit Mobilier* adhered to the essential features of the "*musharaka*" partnership structure. In both cases, profits and losses were shared among the shareholders.

The main purpose of this chapter was to review the milestones in the evolution of risk sharing financial practices from the eleventh to the nineteenth centuries in Europe. From *modaraba* that evolved into *commenda* to the Medicis' methods of financing to those of *Crédit Mobilier*, to the American venture capital financing method, risk sharing modes of innovative financing contributed immensely to the socio-economic development of society. They competed against interest-based debt financing and established an alternative method for mobilizing business capital.

Despite the forceful assault from competitors, these entities contributed to economic growth by financing projects much needed in the society yet not supported by alternative financing methods. Using risk sharing methods, the Medici House, using risk sharing, financed

Florence's artists to craft their masterworks and paintings, and to erect magnificent buildings. Through the use of *commenda*, Venice became a melting pot in which immigrants, natives and traders exchanged music, art, and culture in addition to being a trading hub for the spices and herbs trade. *Crédit Mobilier* financed the grand project of Paris beautification and established the city as the then center of culture and economy. Unfortunately, politics in the service of greed and self-interest conspired to weaken risk sharing in favor of interest rate-based debt. For example, promulgation of regulations, such as the *serrata* in Venice, was clearly intended to put an end to the widespread use of risk sharing instruments through the exercise of power by the ruling elite.

Partnership fostered cohesion among social members and served as an important element of social capital that facilitated expansion of trade and commerce. In finance, partnerships enhanced liquidity for cash-starved artisans and talented young entrepreneurs since it allowed them to share the financial and economic burden of undertakings. Financial contracts promoted coordination, improved corporation, and promoted a sense of security for business dealings as agents sought longer-term relationships. Risk sharing contracts differed significantly from the short-term, interest-bearing loan finance that exploited borrowers' need for liquidity. Partnership financing was an inclusive finance that eased the recovery of society and towns post-crises and allowed the expansion of trade and commerce. The growth of Venice and Florence in the medieval period is evidence of this development.[25]

The important result from utilizing this inclusive financial arrangement was the absence of a dominating power controlling society's resources. Now that city life depended on the cooperation of all citizens; it became a "self-enforcing" institution for generating "*the sense of commonness and*

---

[25] Partnership financing, the rise of middle income class, and increasing level of solidarity are events that preceded city development. In Venetia, *commenda* had empowered the bourgeoisie class to undertake profitable commercial deals. It then led to social movement to remove elites from political power and open the city council for every member of society. The rise of middle-income class also built a social fence and solidarity that repelled the harm from outside the city (de Lara, 2006; Puga & Trefler, 2012). Venetia thus became "*possibly the richest place in the world*" during the Medieval (Acemoglu & Robinson, 2012). In Florence, Medici bank, a rudimentary of joint-stock banks, ventured with small entrepreneurs (such as wool and textile producers). The Medici business model facilitated an upward movement of poor artisans to gain more power in the economy and into the politics (Werveke in Postan et al., 1965, p. 27).

68   P. SWASTIKA AND A. MIRAKHOR

community." In Avner Greif's words: *"Every clan would fight against a renegade clan that attempted to gain political dominance over the city and its economic resources"* (Greif, 2006, p. 176).[26] The only way for allocation of resources was based on public recognition of one's value in honoring trade contracts. De Lara (2006) described these institutions as *"public order, yet reputation-based institutions."* Public-order signified the legal institutions, the law of commerce, and property rights enforcement. Reputation-based authority decided the collective punishment for cheating merchants, dishonored transactions, and other market misconducts. Therefore, the typical public-order, a reputation-based institution, created a system whereby resource allocation was a combined task of both the government and the individuals.

EVOLUTION OF PUBLIC FINANCE INSTRUMENT: PUBLIC FINANCE INSTRUMENTS IN THE EUROPEAN LAND

From late-Antiquity[27] when European lands began to embrace Christianity, the faith slowly imparted its institutions as principles for social life. They comprised the Commandments, the laws, and rulings as the kings' ruling to unify the kingdom and the Church. This "acculturation" or the integration of the faith-based values into the public administration became a directive to organizing life and every part of the social structure. Usury prohibition was one example. The saints and monks strongly condemned interest rate charges on lending transactions, the breach of which eventually led to excommunication from Church and exclusion from society. Overall, the social punishment was severe and shameful for the offender. Consequently, individuals avoided dealing with interest-based loans, including the kings' debt, which was then a "public debt." To avoid the sinful act, kings turned to the monasteries, as the

---

[26] *"This belief and the behaviour it fostered may have helped forge a common Venetian identity that reinforced this belief. In any case, a set of institutionalized rules guided the behaviour of the Venetians toward this self-enforcing belief and generated the conditions required for these beliefs to be self-enforcing... (they even) established tight administrative control over gains from interclan political cooperation, and allocated these rents among all the important Venetian clans so that all had a share in them regardless of clan affiliation"* (Greif, 2006, p. 17).

[27] Late-third century to the mid-seventh century.

latter became kings' lenders and the alternative creditors for long-term loans, as opposed to the usurious moneylenders.[28]

Already in the eighth century, the Carolingian monasteries had invented a financial instrument called "*census.*" *Census* or *rent* was a financial derivative that obtained its value from lease-back contracts registered as the "*precariat*"[29] alternatively, "*beneficium*"[30] estates—lands, villas, and other types of dwelling that landlords voluntarily donated to the church. The principle of the *census* was the return yielded by the "fruits of the properties," such as the rent from endowment assets. Meanwhile, the church received significant endowment assets from individuals whose motivation ranged from religious to economic.[31] It was common for individuals to endow their property to the church. Not to impoverish these people, the church granted them a leaseback contract between the church and the granter for the endowed assets.

The census system became the solution for both parties: the endower kept using the property and the church enjoyed steady annual income. The census was paid annually in perpetuity, sometimes to two lives or more (as stipulated by the church). The *census* sustained the Carolingian economy with a long-term solid flow of payments. Economic stability was then one of the influential factors for socio-economic-political progress

---

[28] The usury or interest ban was also endorsed by the Jewish law, thus disabling the Jewish moneylenders to charge interest on loans. However, the statement in Deuteronomy stipulates the practice to be applicable within the Jewish community, as it says: "*Unto a stranger thou mayest lend upon usury: but unto thy brother thou shalt not lend upon usury.*"

[29] Precariat, came from the Latin verb *precarior* "to beg" or "to pray", is a contract of exchange in which local lords donated vast amounts of their property to monasteries while retaining usufruct of it for themselves and their family in perpetuity (http://www. charlemagneseurope.ac.uk/charter-basics/).

[30] Beneficium, origins from the Latin word means a "favour" or "good deed", is a transaction in which the church granted a person the right to use of an asset once he decided to join the clergy and then immediately receive the use of it back in benefice (Roberts, 2014, http://charlemagneseurope.ac.uk/blog/types-of-charters-2-leases-and-precarial-grants/).

[31] Roberts (2014, http://www.charlemagneseurope.ac.uk/blog/types-of-charter-pro perty-grants/): "*Individuals endowed churches with an eye to the afterlife. They gave to atone for their sins and to please God and his saints... Lay donors might make grants of property to secure clerical or monastic positions for their sons and daughters... Giving to the Church could thus serve as an inheritance strategy which brought families and religious institutions together in mutually beneficial spiritual, economic and political relationship...*".

in Europe.[32] However, the *census* instrument evolved into the *"rente,"* according to which principle was to receive a fixed annual income from selling only the usufruct of its assets while the owner retained the ownership title.

In the twelfth century, *rente* entered the public domain in the European lands. In the center of *Mercato*—the Italian towns Genoa and Venice—government debt came into practice since these cities constantly confronted security issues with their rivals. The instrument served as a source of funding the security protection and building a strong city defense against invaders—it was considered "cheaper" than short-term, interest-bearing loans.

In 1149, and for the first time in Genoa, a consortium of moneylenders took power over a *"compera."* This *compera*, or consolidated fund of tax revenues used for paying the city creditors, was truly a sell contract of receivables. In return, these creditors had to disburse a certain lump sum for the control. According to Macdonald, if the loan was voluntary, the *compera had to be* auctioned; meaning, the highest bidder won the control rights over the designated tax revenues. However, if the loan was mandatory, the payment for the *compera* was divided among society members based on their tax register (Macdonald, 2003, pp. 78–79). This obligation was primarily for a city loan. Since *compera* was recorded in the *"sell-and-buy"* agreement, it connoted with the term "price." Thus, in exchange, the creditor received a predetermined yield that the city allocated from tax receipts.

To render *compera* more appealing, Genoa guaranteed a fixed flow of income from the instrument. It hedged against the risk from a falling sum of the realized tax receipts by farming out tax sources to third parties against a large lump-sum upfront payment. Tax collection through farming—selling the estimated tax revenues on behalf of the authorities, delegating tax collection to a third party, and consenting to the right to keep the collected amounts—was a widespread practice in the Medieval European cities. Farming out tax receipts presented a more efficient method for Genoa since the city lacked the necessary resources for tax collection and often had difficulty dealing directly with taxpayers.

---

[32] Crouzet (2001, p. 6): *"Though Charlemagne's empire remained poor and backward if compared with contemporary China or the Muslim world, some foundations of the European economy were nevertheless laid down from the seventh century to the beginning of the ninth, and the changes that started then were to continue for long afterward."*

Tax farming ensured a steadier flow of income for the city. The revenues safeguarded the fixed payment of *compera* in case the designated tax source did not meet the requirements. It was evident that tax revenues were the payoff source for the city's financial burden that eventually was borne by taxpayers. Consequently, the method of "selling of revenues" became the pattern for several public debt instruments in Medieval Europe.

From the twelfth to fourteenth centuries, Venice was also immersed in creation of a series of "public debts." Initially, like *compera* of Genoa, Venice issued debenture papers as voluntary loans, for which private moneylenders extended city loans at will. In return, the creditors gained control over the tax revenues from the *Rialto* market or the salt tax for a stipulated duration.[33]

In the early thirteenth century, Venice devised "*prestiti*" (forced loan). Like *compera*, the city imposed a premium based on the value of property and assets recorded in the individual's tax register. The city also added an indirect taxe, "*gabella*," to the source for interest payment where it further "*transferred income from the lower- to the upper-income strata*" (Munro, 2003, p. 515). However, unlike in the case of *compera*, Venice developed a secondary market for their *prestiti* where investors, interested in earning a fixed predetermined income, bought the paper at a discount. The mandated *prestiti* was used to strengthen the city's security against foreign invaders that constantly threatened Venice, then the European center of commerce.

In the mid-thirteenth century, Venice finally consolidated its pile of public debt into one large fund (the "*Monte Vecchio*" or the Mountain of Debt) which guaranteed a fixed 5% annual return to the holder. After the public debt consolidation, Venice relinquished its obligation for redemption and shifted the contract to a perpetual liability. The trend of issuing paper debentures, primly for leveling up city security, eventually spread further to other Italian cities, such as Siena and Florence.

During the thirteenth and fourteenth centuries, the usufruct sale was not only practiced in Italy but had become a common instrument

---

[33] Rialto is name of a place that emerged as financial and commercial centre in Venetia. The central government collected commercial tax revenues from merchants who operated his/her businesses on the Rialto market. Salt tax is a charge imposed by the central government upon trading salt as commodities, while the government monopolized the salt production.

for public debt across Europe. Cities and kingdoms, such as Germany, France, and Netherlands, were found to have issued a similar instrument called "*rente*" or "*rent*." *Rente* was a contract by which the issuers sold their future revenues, usually a designated tax source, in exchange for a fixed annual entitlement. Under the terms of the contract, there were two categories of *rente*. First, *the perpetual rent*, also called "*renteheritable*," "*erfelijk rent*," or "*losrent*." As per its name, "*perpetual rent*" provided a permanent, fixed annual payment in perpetuity. It was heritable; after the rentier's death, the rights automatically transferred to his next of kin or close relatives. Second, *the life rente* or "*rent viageere*" or "*lijfrent*." The life rent was a sale contract for future tax receipts entitling *rente* holders to receive an annual payment for as long as they lived. In other words, the right for annuity service extinguished with the licensee's death.

This procedure attracted the attention of the Church and religious scholars. The query was on the legitimacy of the annuities since people subscribed and bought this instrument in pursuit of long-term liquidity and profit. In exchange, the cities, municipalities, kingdoms, or issuers of *Monte* shares or *rente*, all engaged in a long-term "bond," as stipulated in the contract. The features of the instrument made some individuals perceive it as usury, while public authorities wondered whether it was usurious. Social pressures and the Church forewarning of excommunicating people who engaged in usurious transactions nurture people's submission to the Divine Commandments against usury. As more cities issued the debentures and emerged as a system, it naturally caused concerns for the society and the Church.

Monks and religious scholars raised four points of debate: First, whether the contract of "selling for future receivables" (they called it "usufruct" of money) was a legitimate sale contract. Second, whether the yield the buyer received was a licit profit, as rente, thus not usurious, despite the solid return ex ante the real outcome of the sold "assets." Third, the issuer's penalty for pledging all assets to the buyer against services. Fourth, the issuer's right to redemption perceived by the society, like settling the principal payment of a loan contract.

In Italy, the debate had created a conflict between two Catholic orders: The Franciscans and the Dominicans. Francesco da Empoli, the Genoese Franciscan master, issued an edict that differed from that of the latter faith. In his "*Determinatio de Materia Monti*," he approved the transaction as legitimate with the argument that a "*Monte* share" was a purchase of sale of a right to collect future income. Pierro Degli Strozzi, a

Dominican monk, disapproved of this opinion. He saw the selling rights as a way to circumvent usury transaction where the very essence was a similitude of a loan contract. Most Dominicans and Franciscans shared this viewpoint and condemned individual participation in the secondary market in *Crediti di Monte* as *"unnatural and nutritive of sin"* (Munro, 2003, p. 517).[34]

In 1250, William of Rennes, France, issued a ruling on the contract structure that *"renteviagre"* was not usurious as it was not a direct loan contract. He then added the immorality and illegitimacy of the surplus receipt since *rente* was fixed and not based on the performance of the real assets/estates. A year later, in 1251, Pope Innocent IV imposed a strict condition: *rente* could be a legal contract if the annuities were on real asset properties. In Italy, St. Thomas Aquinas extensively discussed the encompassing features of a usurious contract and the social and economic implications of usury in his major work *"Summa Theologica,"* published in the thirteenth century.

In the fifteenth century, in Northern France, the monks Martin V, Nicholas V, and Calixtus III stated in three papal bulls that the legitimacy of *census* or *rente* depend on three conditions: (i) contracts tied to real estate or property; (ii) annuities not to exceed 10% of the capital sum; and (iii) the issuer (borrower) had an unrestricted right of redemption. The third condition referred to the long-term problem of kings or municipalities to redeem the principal amount at maturity that made the contract "appear" like a loan. Redemption was effected at the discretion of the issuer, thus bypassing the core attribute of the loan and ending the restriction.

Fiscal Instruments in the Ottoman Empire

During the sixteenth to the nineteenth centuries, a number of important financial instruments developed in the Muslim regions, particularly those under direct control of the Ottoman Empire. Under the reign of Suleiman I (1520–1566), the Empire was distinguished for its economic superiority and strong military forces. It had conquered vast territories ranging from the Balkans and the Black Sea to the Red Sea and the North

---

[34] Munro (2003, p. 517) added: *"... and those few who merely expressed reservations nevertheless advised everyone 'to refrain from such investments'"*.

74 P. SWASTIKA AND A. MIRAKHOR

Coast of Africa. The empire became the supreme ruler of the conquered Muslim regions.

Population of Turkey itself was composed of a heterogeneous group of people of varied ethnicities and religions. The economy depended on agrarian taxes, where the Sultan, owner of all land, granted farmers and peasants provisions to cultivate the land for periodic tax payments. The vast geographical territory rendered it costly and ineffective for the Sultan and the Central Government to collect directly rents on their resources. They developed the *"Timar"* system. *Timar* system decentralized the tax administration to local areas and authorized local governments and *sipahis*[35] collected the taxes from the peasants. These revenues, in part, were allocated for the purpose of strengthening the local armed forces. In return, provincial governments were obligated to provide stipulated military support to the central government in wartime. Until the late sixteenth century, this *timar* system was sustainable enough to support the Empire in its territorial expansions (Birdal, 2010).

However, the need to upgrade the Empire's armaments created fiscal pressure. The Ottomans' enemies were equipped with more modern weapons and artilleries. Militarization required significant spending that necessitated an innovation in the instrument to increase revenue receipts. Since *timar* did not provide sufficient income, the Central Government initiated *"iltizam,"* or tax farming. It sold off the right to collect taxes to wealthy nobles against a considerable amount of cash advanced to the Sultan. This method was brought about through auction markets where the highest bidder won the entitlement. Wealthy individuals were authorized to collect and keep the tax receivables from a stipulated region and monetary unit for a limited period. The business was lucrative; tax collectors reaped surplus income five times the amount they paid to the Sultan (Duranoglu & Okutucu, 2009). During this period, a new elite class emerged in the social structure, the *"ayans."*

In 1695, the Ottomans introduced another financial instrument called the *"Malikane,"* a modification of the earlier *"iltizam"* tax farm system. The *Malikane system* differed from *iltizam* in the term period. The right to farm taxes under *malikane* system was sold for a lifetime of the buyer/holder. The purchase of *malikane* guaranteed a life fortune for the licensee. Certainly, the price for the longer-term contract was much

---

[35] According to Bridal (2010, p. 19), *sipahis* were civil servants who were mandated to administrate the state land and collect the taxes.

higher than for the shorter term. The Sultan tagged a substantial payment and predetermined annuities for *malikane* with the objective to replace *iltizam* and significantly increase the Central Government revenues. Due to its contract term, the *malikane* system transformed the *iltizam* straight forward short-term tax-farming system into the long-term financing of *malikane* for the Central Government.

However, *malikane* could not raise revenue significantly. The increase in revenue was less than anticipated. Research disclosed that out of 100 *gruş* taxes, the Central Government received only 24 *gruş* (Çizakça, 1996, p. 166). In addition to "insufficient" receipts, the system did not protect taxpayers from the potential harm and greed of tax collectors subcontract the right to third parties. This behavior aggravated the financial burden of taxpayers (Duranoglu & Okutucu, 2009). Contracted parties eyed the surplus of revenue as compensation for their efforts. Karaman and Pamuk (2010) estimated the number of tax collectors and contractors. They found that approximately 1000–2000 collectors were in Istanbul, and 5000–10,000 collectors were actively managing the *malikane* system in the provinces. The regulation and supervision of the system was rather loose and prone to manipulation by corrupt officers. Original buyers passed their *malikane* onto their heirs. Such practices ultimately jeopardized the interest of the Central Government to regain control over the revenue sources after the demise of the tax collectors, leading a long-term loss of income (Çizakça, 1996).

As a result of erosion in the revenue base as well the Empire's defeat in the war against Russia, the Ottoman's Treasury was forced, in the second half of the eighteenth century to design a new fiscal system to increase State revenues and relieve fiscal pressure. The new system, "*esham*," was a lifetime share ownership of estimated annual net income from specified tax sources. Birdal (2010, p. 23) suggests that the Treasury issued *esham* "*to pay for the goods and services for which ready moneycould not be found and for the repayment of short-term loans over longer terms.*" As with *malikane*, the Government designated a special tax source to service the annuity. Whenever revenue was insufficient, payments were made in "*sergis*" (official promise to pay later) (Birdal, 2010).

Collecting taxes, however, continued to be outsourced to tax farmers. The State divided the expected receivables in a considerable number of small-denominated shares and offered the securities to the public at prices five to seven times higher than the annuities. Despite the tagged high price, buyers expected a long-term revenue security from the *esham* since

76   P. SWASTIKA AND A. MIRAKHOR

it guaranteed a continuous flow of income in their lifetime. The pricey *esham* was also a far better bargain than *iltizam* or *malikane*, which enticed individuals who could not participate in purchase of the latter two instruments. The lifetime annuities for the holder were similar to *lijfrente* or *erfelijkrenten*, then popular instruments for public borrowing in Western Europe.

Esham catered to the middle-income investors. Consequently, it was issued in small denominations. It counterbalanced the earlier fiscal system that, allegedly, only benefited certain members of the society. Small-denominated shares attracted many of middle-class individuals and allowed them to diversify their portfolio. The demand was higher for *esham* without *berat* than *esham* with *berat*, because the first granted the right to transfer to other parties. Consequently, the State placed a 10% transaction tax on every transfer which enabled new holders to redeem the benefit (Darling, 2006). This increased the demand for long-term *esham in the secondary market*. As expected, this feature further encouraged people, including women and non-Muslims, to participate in State financing (Darling, 2006, p. 130). Unfortunately, since *malikane* holders had converted to *esham* bearers, it cannot be established concretely that the latter system was more efficient. The presence of a secondary market for *esham* was regarded as the continuous domination of public finances by the upper-income segment of the population since middle-class investors were often unwilling to wait until the maturity date.

Late in the eighteenth century, attempts were made to borrow from external debt market which would have been unprecedented. However, these efforts were unsuccessful.[36] The central government had to turn to the domestic market. This became the motivation for the creation of the *esham*, a financial instrument eliciting wide public participation. The initiative was well- received due to the financial benefits it offered the

---

[36] Pamuk (2007): *"During the war 1787–92 the Ottoman government also considered the possibility of borrowing from abroad, which would have been a first for the Ottoman state, from France, Spain, or Netherlands. In response, the Dutch government indicated in 1789 that it was not able to lend and referred the Ottoman government to the private sector. However, due to difficulties both in Europe arising from the French revolution and the Ottoman side, this possibility could not be pursued any further. Another proposal was to borrow from Morocco because it was a friendly Muslim country, but it was obvious that the ability of Morocco was quite limited…".*

public. Higher public demand for this instrument lowered the cost of financing significantly from 18–19 to 8% (Çizakça, 2013, p. 256).

Worsening economic and financial post-war forced the public to sell the shares of *esham* for quick cash to the renowned financier, the Galata Banker. Moreover, during the mid-nineteenth century, the Government exchanged *esham* for short-term cash borrowed from the Galata Bankers. The interest rate began to soar to 18% and "*could go considerably higher*"[37] (Birdal, 2010, p. 24). This development signaled the beginning of the end of participation-based public finance as *esham* alone became a grossly insufficient instrument to prevent the country from contracting usurious loans. It has been argued that *esham* had become a costly long-term domestic means of financing system. The features, such as selling future revenues, lifetime annuities, and the issuance of perpetual *esham* exacerbated financial difficulties responsible for the Empire's fiscal pressures. The financial costs of these flaws and weaknesses outweighed the benefits of public-based participation instrument.

Allowing public to share risks through participation in government finance was a potent means of reducing the cost of funds and minimizing government's financial and economic risks through pooling and sharing of risks between and among many individuals. However, these benefits were not being considered by Ottoman policymakers upon launching *esham*. Instead, their focus was to offer *esham* to mobilize savings from the middle-income individuals who had been unable to acquire the high-priced *iltizam* or *malikane* instruments (Çizakça, 2013, p. 255). Due to lack of prudent foresight, the Treasury had built features into the *esham* that amplified government's fiscal burden going forward. The budget was overburdened with the cost of servicing annuities, mostly paid in perpetuity. Ultimately, *esham* became an instrument that converted short-term loans to longer-term financing.

It has also been suggested that the real cause of the *esham* failure was the costly wars. It was estimated that, by the time *esham* was introduced, the Empire was in a dire financial situation. The government had to pay 7.5 million *gruş* war indemnity to Russia (Çizakça, 2011). In contrast, it was estimated that the Treasury collected 2 million gruş from *esham* subscriptions in the month of April 1775. Until then, the instrument was

---

[37] These Galata bankers would be willing to pay commission fees for government officers or people from the *paşas* class to ensure the dividend and repayment from *esham* (Birdal, 2010).

successful in generating substantial revenues for the Government. This fact was regarded as one of the instrument's positive features. To sum up, this view argues that war financing was perilous for fiscal management. The funding instruments were unable to ease the financial crisis that resulted from wars; *esham's* impact on the Ottoman economy would have been far more positive under peaceful conditions and proper investments (Çizakça, 2011).

To conclude, this review of public finance instruments from the Medieval Ages to the eighteenth century in the European lands and in the Ottoman Empire demonstrated the core principle of risk sharing public finance in the spirit of achieving common interests without breaching religious commandments. These motives had driven the evolution of the "*Permanently Funded Public Debt*" (PFPD) instruments. The method specified the time-span of instruments, from short-term to long-term contracts, based on government's need—the larger the amount, the longer the contract term. From *census* to *compera* and *rente* to Ottoman *timar, iltizam, malikane*, and *esham*, local and national governments used these instruments to cover their expenses, mainly fortifying their armies for defense or financing costly wars.

In the beginning, public finance instruments issued by city-states distributed these costs among the people. The city collected money from the people for erecting defense walls or financing battles against enemies. At first, the collection was voluntary but later was made compulsory; rulers stipulated the amount. In the process, total spending surged and it was sold as debentures. In exchange, the people who provided financing received control over future revenues, extracted from a stipulated tax basket. The tax system was also intended to increase people's participation in the city's organization for safety and security. People agreed to subscribe to public finance instruments and pay taxes to cover the costs of defending their lands. As a result of the growth of expenditures—far beyond tax capacity or direct public participation via purchase of revenue-expenditure sharing instruments—governments resorted to simpler method of interest-rate-based borrowing thus transferring/shifting the burden of the growing expenditures to the present and future taxpayers. In time, risk transfer/shifting method of financing became entrenched in economies.

From the Late Antiquity to the nineteenth century, public loan contracts had evolved or had transformed to assume different structures—leaseback contract and sell-off of future revenues (or receivables)—to circumvent religious, moral and ethical rules. Such instrument created an enormous burden for the budget because of the way these instruments were structured and designed. In essence, they were interest-based debt securities; a fact that was not immediately evident. The interest-rate system decoupled risks from a licit profit and converted financial risk to uncertainty. The alternative system that required risk distribution among participants according to their ability to bear risks operated under the principle *"ubi non estmutuum, ibi non estusura,"*[38] or under the commandment that *"Allah has made Al-Bay' permissible and Ar-Riba unlawful."*[39]

REFERENCES

Acemoglu, D., & Robinson, J. A. (2012). *Why nations fail: The origins of power, prosperity, and poverty*. Crown.

Baskin, J. B., & Miranti, P. J. (1997). *A history of corporate finance*. Cambridge University Press.

Birdal, M. (2010). *The political economy of Ottoman public debt: Insolvency and European financial control in the late nineteenth century*. I. B. Tauris.

Cameron, R. E. (1953). The credit mobilier and the economic development of Europe. *The Journal of Political Economy, LXI*(6), 461–488.

Cameron, R., & Bovykin, V. I. (1991). *International banking 1870–1914* (R. Cameron & V. I. Bovykin, Eds.). Oxford University Press.

Çizakça, M. (1996). *A comparative evolution of business partnerships: The Islamic world and Europe, with specific reference to The Ottoman Archives*. Brill Academic.

Çizakça, M. (2006). Cross-cultural borrowing and comparative evolution of institutions between islamic world and the west. In S. Cavaciocchi (Ed.), *Relazioni economiche tra Europa e mondo Islamico* (Secc. XIII–XVIII). Prato.

Çizakça, M. (2011). *Islamic capitalism and finance: Origins, evolution and the future*. Edward Elgar.

Çizakça, M. (2013). *The Ottoman government and economic life: Taxation, public finance, and trade controls*. Cambridge University Press.

Crouzet, F. (2001). *A history of the European economy, 1000–2000*. The University Press of Virginia.

---

[38] Quoted from the Leuven theologian Leonardius Lessius (d. 1623) as cited from de Roover (1969) in Munro (2003, p. 523) that translates "where there is no loan there is no usury."

[39] The Holy Quran (S2:275).

Darling, L. T. (2006). Public finances: The role of the Ottoman centre. *The Cambridge History of Turkey, 3*, 118–131.

de Aghion, B. A. (1999). Development banking. *Journal of Development Economics, 58*, 83–100.

de Lara, Y. G. (2006). The secret of venetian success: Public-order yet reputation-based institutions. In *XIV International Economic History Congress*. Helsinki.

de Roover, R. (1963). *The rise and decline of the Medici Bank, 1297–1494*. Harvard University Press.

Drucker, P. F. (1998). The discipline of innovation. *Harvard Business Review*.

Duranoglu, E., & Okutucu, G. (2009). *Economic reasons behind the decline of the Ottoman empire*.

Easterly, W., & Stiglitz, J. E. (2000). *Shaken and stirred: Explaining growth volatility* (pp. 1–13). Mimeo.

Eckalbar, J. C. (1979). The Saint-Simonians in industry and economic development. *The American Journal of Economics and Sociology, 38*(1), 83–96.

Glaisyer, N. (2006/2008). *The culture of commerce in England, 1660–1720* (x + 220 pp. $75 [cloth]). Boydell Press. ISBN: 0-86193-281-1.

Greif, A. (1994). On the political foundations of the late medieval commercial revolution: Genoa during the twelfth and thirteenth centuries. *Journal of Economic History, 54*, 271–287.

Greif, A. (2006). *Institutions and the path to the modern economy: Lessons from medieval trade*, 1–31.

Harris, R. (2000). *Industrializing English Law*. https://doi.org/10.1017/CBO9780511510137.

Harris, R. (2009). The institutional dynamics of early modern Eurasian trade: The commenda and the corporation. *Journal of Economic Behavior and Organization*. https://doi.org/10.1016/j.jebo.2009.04.016.

Karaman, K. K., & Pamuk, S. (2010). Ottoman state finances in comparative European perspective, 1500–1914. *The Journal of Economic History, 70*(3), 593–627.

Khalilieh, H. S. (2006). *Admiralty and maritime laws in the Mediterranean Sea (ca. 800-1050)*. Leiden: Brill.

Lopez, R. S. (1976). *The commercial revolution of the middle ages, 950–1350*. Cambridge University Press.

Macdonald, J. (2003). *A free nation deep in debt: The financial roots of democracy*. New York: Farrar, Straus and Giroux.

Mathias, P., & Postan, M. M. (1978). *The Cambridge economic history of Europe, the industrial economics: Capital, labour, and enterprise, Part I: Britain, France, Germany, and Scandinavia*, Vol. III. Cambridge at the University Press.

Mian, A., & Sufi, A. (2014). *House price gains and U.S. household spending from 2002 to 2006* (National Bureau of Economic Research Working Papers No. 20152 May).

Munro, J. H. (2003). The medieval origins of the financial revolution: Usury, rentes, and negotiability. *International History Review, XXV*, 505–756.

Neal, L., & Schubert, E. S. (1985). *The first rational bubbles: A new look at the Mississippi and South Sea schemes.*

Newmarch, W. (1858). On the recent history of the credit mobilier. *Journal of the Statistical Society of London, 21*(4), 444–453.

Newton, L. (2007). *Change and continuity: The development of joint stock banking in the early nineteenth century.* Centre for International Business History. University of Reading.

Ng, A., Mirakhor, A., & Ibrahim, M. H. (2015). *Social capital and risk sharing: An Islamic finance paradigm.* Palgrave Macmillan.

North, D. C. (1991). Institutions and productivity in history. In *Institutions, transaction costs and the rise of merchant empires* (pp. 1–13).

Norwich, J. J. (1977). *Venice: The rise to empire.* Allen Lane.

Pamuk, Ş. (2007). From debasement to external borrowing: Changing forms of deficit finance in the Ottoman empire, 1750–1914. *Monetary and Fiscal Policies in South-East Europe, 7.*

Paulet, E. (1999). *The role of banks in monitoring firms: The case of the crédit mobilier* (1st ed.). Routledge.

Piketty, T. (2014). *Capital in the twenty-first century.* Harvard University Press.

Poitras, G. (2016). *Equity capital: From ancient partnerships to modern exchange traded funds.* Routledge (US). ISBN: 9781138819931.

Postan, M. M., Rich, E. E., & Miller, E. (1965). *The Cambridge economic history of Europe: Economic organization and policies in the middle ages.* Cambridge: Cambridge University Press.

Puga, D., & Trefler, D. (2012). *International trade and institutional change: Medieval Venice's response to globalization* (No. 9076).

Reinhart, C., & Rogoff, K. (2009). *This time is different.* Princeton University Press.

Roberts, E. (2014). *Types of charters 2: Leases and precarial grants.*

Scott, W. R. (1912). *The constitution and finance of English, Scottish, and Irish joint-stock companies to 1720.* Mass. P. Smith.

Smith, M. S. (2006). *The emergence of modern business enterprise in France, 1800–1930 (Harvard St).* Harvard University Press.

Udovitch, A. L. (1962). At the origins of the Western Commenda: Islam, Israel, Byzantium? *Speculum, 37*(2), 198–207. https://doi.org/10.2307/3210793.

Walsh, R. H. (1856). *Notes on the Société Générale de Crédit Mobilier.*

Weber, M., & Kaelber, L. (2003). *The history of commercial partnerships in the middle ages.*

Zouache, A., & Boureille, B. (2009). How to coordinate economic activities in a social order: An essay on the Saint-Simonian economic doctrine (1825–1832). *History of Economic Ideas, 17*(2), 65–76.

CHAPTER 5

The Foundation of the German Economy: Concept and Practices

This chapter highlights theories, ideas, and policies implemented by the German economy from the nineteenth century up to the Great Depression in 1929 which established the foundation for market rules (institutions). They represented standards and norms of behavior, perceptible in practices and methods. Institutions changed, and so did practices and methods. This chapter centers on the principle that past events affect future decisions.

UP TO THE NINETEENTH CENTURY

Trading was an integral element of the German economy. In the nineteenth century, urban development throughout Germany integrated cities and active trading. Merchants of the Hansa States along the Rhine-Danube were reputable sailors and traders. The trader guilds imposed the requirement of compliance with institutions (coordination, commitment, and rule-enforcement) when choosing the members of their organization from small, middle-sized merchants. The organization safeguarded merchants' rights of property and provided them with a trade network in the Hansa League for the exchange of goods. The guilds accepted membership applications from candidates who were committed to the rules of shared-interest and freedom to trade for the

© The Author(s), under exclusive license to Springer Nature Switzerland AG 2021
P. Swastika and A. Mirakhor, *Applying Risk-Sharing Finance for Economic Development*, Political Economy of Islam, https://doi.org/10.1007/978-3-030-82642-0_5

84 P. SWASTIKA AND A. MIRAKHOR

guilds' success. Membership was voluntary, and equality sealable by oath (Wubs-Mrozewicz, 2013). The middle-class merchants enjoyed unity and security against threats and domination by wealthy traders.

For trade, middle-class merchants favored partnership contracts. They used and shared two traits in partnership: (i) "*Sendegeschäft*" or "*Send even*;" (ii) "*Wiederlegung*" or "*Wederlegginge*," known in southern Germany as "*Fürlegung*"[1] (de Lara, 2003, p. 481; Postan, 1973, pp. 70–71). What distinguished *Sendegeschäft* from *Wiederlegung* was the nature of partnership or risk sharing. *Sendegeschäft* (goods sent out) implied a silent partnership. Capital owners entrusted their resources to merchants without their involvement. Entrepreneurs directed their efforts, time, and skills to actively conduct their business. On the other hand, *Wiederlegung* was an active partnership, where all parties shared capital and entrepreneurship. In *Wiederlegung*, the merchants shared the risks according to their capital contribution.[2] In *Sendegeschäft*, capital owners carried all the risk while the merchants lost only time and efforts.

---

[1] *Wiederlegung* (or *Wederlegginge*) was associated with the standard unilateral *Commenda*. *Sendegeschäft* is comparable to *societasmaris*, but in a way that the capital provider entrusted goods for sale to the merchant's partners. Both *Wiederlegung* and *Sendegeschäft* were more typical contracts employed rather than loans by the merchants in the Hansa cities.

(*"In the Hanseatic cities, the two most significant contracts of the collaboration of capital with labour were the Sendegesgeschäft and the Wiederlegung. It is interesting to compare these typical contracts of the ports of the Mediterranean, the command, and the "societasmaris." It should be noted, according to these documents, the participation of the two parties in the capital were more frequent in the north, as in Venice (collegantia), than in Genoa, Marseilles, and Barcelona*," André Sayous, 1936, p. 193).

(*"Dans les villes hanséatiques, les deux contrats principaux de collaboration du capital avec le travail étaient le Sendegeschäft et la Wiederlegung qu'il est intéressant de rapprocher de deux contrats typiques des ports de la Méditerranée, la commande et la societasmaris. Observons, de suite, que d'après les documents que la visent, que la participation des deux parties en capital a été plus fréquente dans le Nord, comme à Venise (collegantia), qu'à Gênes, Marseille et Barcelone...*," André Sayous, 1936, p. 193).

[2] Found in *Wiederlegung*, it consisted of two merchants, both contributed trading capital in the ratio of 1:1 or 2:1. In the case of 2:1 ratio, the merchant with a bigger contribution received the first- third part of the proceeds and the remainder of third-fourth was shared between the two merchants. Loss ratio was according to the capital portion. It is worth noting that in *Wiederlegung*, the works carried by the agents were not considered "capital contribution" (Punt, 2010).

The commercial contract initiated an economy with community responsibility as its pillar.[3] In this community, social cohesion was essential for guaranteeing successful business transactions. In the absence of a government, community oversight posed as market regulator and rules enforcer. The system also promoted better distribution of social welfare. As early as the twelfth and thirteenth centuries, German mine-workers shared in the company's liabilities by contributing their labor for profit sharing. This traditional risk sharing model evolved into *Kuxen*, first known in the fifteenth century. *Kuxen* was similar to the modern definition of stocks, as it represented ownership and rights to earn dividends from the mining company.[4] By the sixteenth century, capital markets widely employed and traded *Kuxen* and regarded them as a practical measure to limit investors' business losses (Kensinger & Poe, 2005).

The socio-political crisis of the seventeenth century, however, halted the economic progress. The political and religious revolts in important European cities disturbed commercial activities in the European land. In Germany, the seventeenth century represented the rise of the Lutheran movement and the Thirty-Year War against the Protestants. Civil conflicts and upheavals adversely affected trade but not in all towns. Cities like Hamburg and North-Western Germany remained safe and prosperous. They benefited from their falling neighbors. Further, their local authority pledged to provide security for distressed merchants and markets. The fall of Lübeck, the capital of the Hansa League, helped Hamburg to emerge as global marketplace after London and Amsterdam (Lindberg, 2008). Studies have explained that strong regulation was one reason for

[3] The community responsibility system is a system where community is held liable for a member's default in intercommunity exchange. The system is observed in historical documents (charters) and imperial laws enacted in Europe, such as Italy, England, Germany and the Hanseatic League during the late Medieval period. Unlike England, where the State replaced the community responsibility system with individual legal responsibility and State power. However, German towns fulfilled the collective responsibility system until the sixteenth century (Greif, 2006, p. 343).

[4] When mines and minerals became harder to find, workers had to contribute more than their labour. They had to dig the galleries, invest in machineries such as props, winding-gear, and water drainer that needed to be built below the surface. This situation opened the door for *Kuxen* as a financing method so that merchants, being the capital owner, could be associated with the mines but distanced from the daily operation (Braudel, 1982, p. 322). The division of the shares, however, was based on abstract calculation. Ulrich Rüleinwrote in his book **Bergbüchlein**, "...One *Kuxen* is worth 128 shares ("... *ein Kucks ist einhundertachtundtzwentzig Teil*..." (Connolly, 2005, p. 642, Appendix A.).

Hamburg's rise as a commercial center.[5] This power-sharing-based constitution became evidence for the city's development to a central trade hub amid the seventeenth-century crisis.[6]

Meanwhile, scholars considered the study of the economy of the eighteenth century as a branch of learning. They conceptualized it as a distinct branch of philosophy, taught as one corpus. The meaning of economics differed sharply from today's conception because scholars subdivided it under three categories: "*Ökonomie*," "*Polizei*," and "*Cameralwissenschaften*." Each category carried a different meaning. *Ökonomie* for promoting individual happiness, *Polizei* for promoting general happiness, and *Cameralwissenschaft*, a combination of both ideas summed in "*gute Polizei*."[7] As early as the eighteenth century, German scholars adduced that economics was about studying the ways and means of achieving individual and general happiness anchored by coordinated actions following the order of the State.[8]

---

[5] It is known that the most important market for *Kuxen* was in Leipzig fair. During the sixteenth and seventeenth centuries, Leipzig became the most important *Messe Stadt* (trade fair) than other German cities, such as Nuremberg, Augsburg, or even Frankfurt am Main. Braudel quotes (1982, p. 189): "*Leipzig succeeded in capturing the mines of Germany, attracting the most important market in Kuxen (mining shares) to the city, and setting up direct links with Hamburg and the Baltic, which was weaned away from its previous way-station of Magdeburg. But it also remained firmly attached to Venice, 'Venice goods' propped up an entire sector of its activity. Leipzig also became par excellence the transit station for goods travelling between East and West.... In 1710, it could be argued that the Leipzig fairs were 'more important and considerable' than those of Frankfurt, at least for commodities, for the city on the Main was still, at this period, a financial Centre of much greater importance than Leipzig.*"

[6] Hamburg's 1529 Constitution had two important consequences: First, it formally recognized a few institutions governed by merchants and artisans. Second, it explicitly defined a balance of power between different city groups, most importantly, between the burghers and the council. No single party could monopolize political power (Lindberg, 2008, pp. 654–655).

[7] Unlike Lübeck or Danzig, Hamburg was the melting pot of international merchants. It conceded freedom of religion and commercial liberty. Power-sharing institutions "forced" the city to grant no privileges or special treatment to certain groups or merchants in the market (Lindberg, 2008, p. 656).

[8] Based on the above, *Cameralism* dealt mainly with state administration, while *Ökonomie* debated achieving the objective of happiness, and *Polizei* was concerned with the general state order in Tribe (1995, p. 11).

Friedrich List, a renowned economist of the nineteenth century, launched the Customs Union "*Zollverein*"[9] and the Railways Center. His vision was to reduce transaction costs within the country. For Germany, then divided into States under different sovereigns, customs unions and connected transport would boost trade and spur the economy. List considered the Union balanced the interest of importers and local producers and contributed to an ideal economic arrangement for both parties.[10] This view centered on equality—free trade would be legitimate, furthering economic progress, only if everyone had equal access to the resources of production. If this was not possible, the authorities were to safeguard the interests of local producers before competing with imported goods. The *Zollverein* proposal passed in 1834, becoming an important model of early economic integration.

In 1833, List also proposed the first railway's construction in Germany. He wrote his idea in a book "*On the Saxony Railway System as a Foundation of a General German Railway-System.*" List asserted the importance of setting up this new transport system to allow economic progress and attaining to additional social benefits for the community.[11] The book not only detailed the proposal but also offered a farsighted proposal for financing the project. He explained the financing structure for the project and estimated profits to the State of Sachsen if the project was performed as planned. List purposely suggested the use of stocks as the source of funding as demonstrated in the railway construction plan of

---

[9] The German economy was based on values that considered wealth and happiness as the outcome of social relations. Therefore, economic order was not enforced by authority or the State. The State organized "the laws of motion" inherent in the society (Tribe, 1995, pp. 30–31). An example of such economy was the public finance of Hohenzollern Prussia, where the State adhered to parsimonious "*Hausvater*" finance principle "*living within one's means,*" which was noticeable in an agrarian economy.

[10] *Zollverein* or Customs Union was a union for all German States, including Luxemburg that shared the same intentions to secure complete freedom of internal trade and to establish a single tariff on imports. The revenue from import duties was divided according to the population of each State which is a member of the Union. Since the establishment of the Union, there was great expansion in Germany's industry, agriculture, and commercial activities.

[11] List wrote: "*I would indicate, the distinguishing characteristic of my system is Nationality. On the nature of nationality, as the intermediate interest between those of individualism and of entire humanity, my whole structure is based*" (List, 1885, p. xliii).

North America and England.[12] He emphasized that equity financing would further the organization because the shares' limited liability would protect shareholders and the State from losing critical projects while having enhanced oversight of management's performance. The book was farsighted and innovative; it considered the unity and connectedness among States as considerable progress of civilization.[13]

At the beginning of construction, the company introduced an innovative financing instrument—the "railway notes." The notes connoted "equity paper"—exchangeable only for railways services. These notes financed one-third of the costs of construction. Zander (1933) noted:

"... *Friedrich List, just a century ago, built the Leipzig-Dresden Railway, he approved to issue 500,000 Thaler—one-third of the Company's capital—in the form of "railway moneycertificates, subject to the provision that no duty would arise from that place to the State."*

The certificate directed the issuing party, the railway company, to dispense the note as a share in the company's ownership. The company offered the note to suppliers and contractors in exchange for their services. It also recognized the validity of the notes and guaranteed their value based on the indicated nominal amount. This amount was

---

[12] List wrote: "*Increasing the population and industry, on the other hand, will increase the rent and, consequently, the value of the buildings well situated in the city to trade and commerce. In one word, population, number of buildings, trade-industry, commerce, and Leipzig's house and land values would be doubled in a brief time. I doubt not for a moment that this value increase in Leipzig alone would far exceed the capital employed on railways in a few years.*"

"*...Vermehrung der Bevölkerung und der Gewerbe dagegen werden die Mietzins und folglich den Wert der zu Handel und Gewerbe gut gelegenen Gebäude im Innern der Stadt erhöhen. Mit einem Wort: Bevölkerung, Gebäudezahl, Gewerbs-Industrie, Handel und Wert der Häuser und Grundstücke von Leipzig würden sich in kurzer Zeit verdoppeln, und ich zweifle keinen Augenblick, daß diese Wertvermehrung in Leipzig allein das auf die Eisenbahnen verwendete Kapital in wenigen Jahren weit übersteigen würde*" (List, 1833, p. 21).

[13] List marked the use of stocks to finance railroad project in the US and England. The projects were executed without the state's financial support. Further references on the US railroad construction appears in the book by Charles Francis Adams, Jr., "*Railroads: Their Origin and Problems* (1878, reprinted in 1981) and Dobbin and Dowd (1997), "*How Policy Shapes Competition: Early Railroad Founding in Massachusetts,*" for a quality reference of states policy in using public funds to found railway industry (public capitalization policy regime) in Massachusetts railroading, and Forrester (2006), "*The General Steam Navigation Company c. 1850–1913: A Business History,*" for a general account on stock financing for steamship and railway companies in England.

redeemable for railway services, in general, but not for cash. Since the notes were only for exchange, they were issued in small denominations. Consequently, a secondary market accepted and traded the notes for instant cash to cover the gap in transactions. The market established the rate of return based on supply and demand.[14] This method succeeded in advocating the Leipzig-Dresden line as an alternative for small investors. However, after over forty years of circulation, the issuing of these notes had to stop in late nineteenth century when the Reich Treasury issued its own notes.

This method marked a significant aspect of financing public projects. An alternative means of exchange was feasible, provided the value of the railway notes remained stable. In addition to its warranty, being convertible to railway services (asset-backed) and the convenience of a secondary market also influenced the value of the note. The secondary market confirmed the paper's value and attractiveness for investment. This railway notes also allowed private businesses (suppliers and contractors) to engage in public projects without the State's interest-rate bearing bonds—an important message that their contribution would assist regional economic development. Again, risk sharing principles had confirmed the strong link between financial reform and socio-economic development. Here, the railway notes promoted technology and transport progress that, in turn, prompted development of Germany.[15]

---

[14] Railways construction was the hallmark of the nineteenth century's industrialization era in Western Europe, particularly in Germany. It had evidently made the distribution of iron materials and mines quicker and easier, and thus positively contributed to "technological import" of modern technology to Germany. As quoted in Da Rin (1997, p. 186) that 60% of domestic production of locomotives were made in Germany by the year 1852. According to Riesser (1911, p. 34), there were several railways projects that significantly improved domestic economic. These were: the Nuremberg-Fürth railway (1835); the Berlin-Potsdam, and the Braunschweig-Wolfenbüttel lines (1838); the Leipzig-Dresden line (1839); the Leipzig-Magdeburg, the München-Augsburg, the Mannheim-Heidelberg, and the Frankfurt-Mainz lines (1840); and the Berlin-Anhalt, the Düsseldorf-Elberfeld, and the Cologne-Elberfeld railways (1841).

[15] Zander (1933, p. 358) wrote: "*Should the market rate fall below the nominal value—say to 95% thereof—everybody who desires to travel or forward goods by rail would be eager to acquire certificates, for the Railway is obliged to accept the latter at their face value. The holder of the railway money (prospective passenger or forwarder) may thus save 5% of his railway expenses. The attractiveness of the certificates thus grows as their value drops and, accordingly, a fall in their value stimulates the demand for them. In turn, the growing demand will raise the market rate until the nominal value is reached, when the demand will slacken. An open market for the railway money guarantees therefore its soundness.*"

Joint-stock banking system soon followed the railroad development. In the 1850s, *"Die Bank für Handel und Industrie"* or *"Die Darmstädter Bank,"* occupied a central role in the industrialization (Cameron, 1953, p. 465). The pattern shortly became the prototype of banks and other organizations. The number of new joint-stock banks mushroomed. From 1851 to 1870, the number of joint-stock companies swelled: from only 102 companies with total capital of 38 million marks to 295 businesses with a total of 2.405 trillion marks in Prussia (Riesser, 1911, p. 38). Moreover, according to Cameron (1953), the *"A. Schaffhausen Bankverein"* of Cologne, the *"Discontogesellschaft,"* and all important German banks copied the joint-stock model of the *"Darmstädter Bank."*

The German banking system in the 1850s was influenced by the French joint-stock bank *"Credit Mobilier"* which took part in establishing the *Darmstädter Bank*, which allowed it to appoint one of their high-ranking bankers to the management of the *Darmstädter Bank*.[16] The *Darmstädter Bank* business model resembled the system followed by *Credit Mobilier*.[17] Their statutes rested on the mandate to conduct "entrepreneurial tasks." To that end, the bank was to get involved in promoting new companies, merging or consolidating different companies, and transforming industrial undertakings into common stocks projects. *"Disconto Gesellschaft"* and the *Darmstädter Bank* also extended their activity as underwriters, engaged in shares issuance or acquisition

---

[16] Many economic historians attributed the socio-economic progress of the nineteenth century Western Europe and England to the "seemingly-impossible" projects in technology and transportation systems, particularly the establishment of steam ships and railways. The progress improved the flow of trade, facilitated migration and people's movement from one place to another, decreased transportation costs for goods and people, and created a transformation in the civilization as people gathered and knowledge spread easier. These factors contributed to reform in many industrial branches, including the banking business. The banking industry became more open to alternative financing methods, such as equity-financing and other types of risk sharing arrangement. As a result, the joint stock company proved to be *"the most reliable ally of trade and industry, conducted on a large scale, and necessary for transforming private concerns into joint stock companies and establishing new industrial enterprises in the shape of stock companies...,"* as quoted in Riesser (1911, p. 4).

[17] According to Riesser (1911, pp. 49–50) one of the co-founders of the *Darmstädter Bank* was also the founders of *Credit Mobilier*, Abraham Oppenheim of Cologne. He, thus, was among the first directors of the *Darmstädter Bank* who came from the higher officials of the *Credit Mobilier*.

of company debentures (Whale, 1930, p. 12)—a sharp contrast to the conventional business of other private bankers.

A feature differentiating German joint-stock banks from the French model was the involvement in State financing. At their inception, German joint-stock banks engaged in government financing. Unlike *Credit Mobilier*, which focused on funding railways and industrial transactions, German joint-stock banks had appointed a special body mandated to participate in the financing of government activities. This action was undertaken in order to functionally separate the risks of financing private and public sectors within the asset portfolio of banks. Another feature of the German banks was that they never engaged with an unlimited capital contribution to their subsidiary or affiliated companies. They also stipulated strict conditions for deposit activities.[18]

Promoting industries became a customary practice for German banks. When they did not contribute to the company's capital, the banks nevertheless induced entrepreneurs to direct their idle capital to enterprises. Further, they pledged their expertise in management to supervise the invested funds. The Germans easily accepted joint-stock banks because of their inclusive nature. Under the system, entrepreneurs unable to procure financing from lenders could mobilize the needed financing by appealing to small savers. These competitive institutions managed to reduce the power of traditional private bankers over industries, such as in the railway construction.

The direct participation allowed money to circulate more effectively. The old banking business lacked this advantage since the wealthy maintained their private property over the money they lent, with the help of laws, even when borrowers were unable to meet the stipulated condition of the predetermined interest rate. Under the traditional system, banks ignored developmental projects that were not operating on predetermined, fixed interest rate. This created an advantage for joint-stock banks,

---

[18] Like *Credit Mobilier*, the *Darmstädter Bank* founded new companies, among which were: the *Wollmanufaktur Mannheim* (paid-up share capital 400.000 florins), the *Württembergische Kattunmanufaktur* (paid-up share capital 500.000 florins), the *Oldenburgische Ostindische Reederei* (paid-up share capital 250.000 florins), the *Kammgarnspinnerei und Weberei, Marklissa* (paid-up share capital 300.000 florins), the *Ludwigshütte*, near Biedenkopf (paid-up share capital 360.000 thalers, jointly with the *Mitteldeutsche Kreditbank*), and involved in the formation of *Maschienenfabrik und Eisengiesserei Darmstadt* as a joint-stock company (paid-up capital 200.000 florins) and the *HeilbronnerMaschienenbaugesellschaft* (Riesser, 1911, p. 63).

allowing a distinctive contribution to economic development. Joint-stock banks allocated depositors' savings to productive projects, mostly construction such as bridges, canals, and transportation that produced new demands in the labor market, thus generating employment and income. The increase in income and employment rates resulted in a general improvement of the economic conditions. The two features of joint-stock banks were: (i) a more efficient capital mobilization, and (ii) a sustainable capital flow within the market. Both features motivated the public to contribute even more to the national economy.[19] To some extent, the firm link between banks and industries exists to date in the German banking system.

THE EARLY TWENTIETH CENTURY

Before WWI, the German Empire adopted a monetary system based on fractional gold reserves.[20] This system soon supported the rearmament program, which led to large fiscal deficits and, eventually, to depreciation. The "*Reichsbank*" financed government deficits by absorbing the short-term Treasury Bills and war bonds. Under fractional reserves, this short-term T-Bills (*Schatzanweisungen*) constituted the entire portfolios of the Reichsbank and financial institutions. The situation revealed that war financing depleted the country's reserves, which caused people, under the circumstances, to reduce spending and increase savings.

In the early twentieth century, Silvio Gesell, a German manufacturer, wrote on an alternative monetary system. In his book, published in 1918

---

[19] When paying deposit, it was specified that depositors should not expect an appreciable increase from the bank during the saving period and that they must provide a withdrawal notice within the agreed period. It was quoted from the report of the Schaffhausen Bankverein in 1856; "*We do not consider it desirable in the interests of the complete security of our institution to attract increased deposits by offering favourable terms, since we prefer, so far as is compatible with the nature of banking business and the interests of our customers (correspondents) to carry on our business with our resources*" (Whale, 1930, pp. 14–15).

[20] The German banking system continued to develop in the beginning of twentieth century, but activities slowly decayed in the years prior to World War I. Apart from the opportunity of promoting new ventures, the unification of Germany expanded the opportunity for banks to open branches (*Filialen*) and groups in other regions. It also pushed for an integration of the banking system, which took Berlin as the financial centre, to which joint-stock banks gradually moved their headquarters, including the headquarters of the Reichsbank (*Reichsbankhauptstelle*).

and titled "*The Natural Economic Order*," Gesell argued that the problem of the conventional monetary system was the interest-rate mechanism. Interest rate created circulation problem and considered money as an object of trading. The system induced hoarding and speculation. He also condemned the gold standard because the issues of money pegged to gold were economically unjust—gold did not increase in productive capacity. The conventional financial system created a separate arena for the financial market vis-à-vis the real sector. In his book, he explained that a producer or entrepreneur had to bear "the storage costs" of inventories and goods from a real economic sector, while the interest rate was a pecuniary incentive for holding onto liquidity. Gesell hinted at this problem by pointing to the liquidity preference phenomenon, whereby agents preferred money to real assets.

This interest-rate paradigm subverted the genuine purposes of a monetary system. The system was supposed to facilitate financial market activities in tandem with real sector production. Banks and financial institutions indulged in money-to-money transactions but were reluctant in promoting production, exchange and trade transactions. Undertaking the financing of projects in the real sector required greater effort in monitoring and exercising oversight as compared to money-money financial transaction. Hence, the ease of interest-rate debt became much more attractive and laid the foundation for the dominance of risk transfer and risk shifting finance.

To create incentives for risk sharing and discouraging risk transfer, Gesell suggested charging a storage cost for holding money. He proposed the "money stamp" (*Zahlungsakte*) or "surcharges" (*Zuschlagsätze*) to remove the positive return to money transactions and encourage a more rapid circulation. According to Gesell, these surcharges would force the rentier class or "the capitalist"[21] to void hoarding which was counterproductive to economic progress. Surcharging, however, was simple.

---

[21] On July 31, 1914, because of depleted gold reserve, the Reichsbank suspended the conversion of currency to gold in great quantities. On August 4, a law supporting the Act of July 31 was issued. On the same date, another law authorized the Reichsbank to discount short-term Treasury bills and to use these bills (incl. commercial bills) as backing for the currency (Bresciani Turroni, 1968, p. 23). In August 1914, the gold reserves system was relinquished, allowing T-bills and other government bonds (of no more than three months) to run as a legal backing for the currency (Schacht as quoted in Northrop, 1938, p. 26, footnote 1).

If monetary authority declared that money would lose 1/1000 (one-thousandth) of its nominal value (or about 5% per annum), and if the holders wished to keep the face value of the notes, they had to pay the stamps fees at otherwise diminished value at the end of every month through financial institutions. If the holder did not or forgot to buy the stamps, then their money holding would lose part of its nominal value. Therefore, when interest rate imparted positive value to money, Gesell's proposal placed money in a position to lose its value progressively. Accordingly money would depreciate as would physical assets.

Over time, Gesell's vision and the proposal received much abuse and criticism. He was called "the monetary crank" (Garvy, 1975) and several conventional economists ridiculed his ideas. It took at least two decades for renowned economists, such as Irving Fisher and John Maynard Keynes, to view Gesell's proposal positively. Irving Fisher, in his book "*Booms and Depressions*" (1932), praised the money stamp as "*the most efficient method of controlling hoarding and probably the speediest way out of depression.*" John Maynard Keynes took a different course. Unlike Fisher who supported the Stamp Money, Keynes complimented Gesell's vision but declared that imposing the depreciating money was not possible. Keynes wrote in "*General Theory of Employment, Money, and Interest*" (1936): "*It is convenient to mention at this point the strange, unduly neglected prophet Silvio Gesell, whose work contains flashes of deep insight and who only just failed to reach down to the essence of the matter... Nevertheless, he had carried his theory far enough to lead him to a practical recommendation, which may carry with it the essence of what is needed, though it is not feasible in the form in which he proposed it*" (Keynes, 1936, pp. 322–325).

To sum, Gesell's vision was to promote an efficient monetary system that emphasized real asset transactions as essential for economic growth. He opposed "the capitalist' or 'the rentier" class who treated money as a category of assets. His argument was that such behavior would disrupt the flow of financial resources to the real sector. He viewed continuous circulation and capital mobilization for the real sector as necessary for maintaining a healthy economy. A solution was needed that would dissuade hoarding and speculation and reorient the system toward promoting the real sector of the economy. Gesell's proposal was to subject money holdings to the process of depreciation.

In 1919, Germany had lost the war and depleted its financial resources. The Treaty of Versailles destroyed the morale of the people who regarded the Treaty as a psychological shock to the pride of their country. Gottfried Feder came to public attention through his strong views against the interest rate system. As mentioned in the Introduction, disheartened by the war defeat and the Treaty of Versailles, Feder expressed his views in a small book entitled "*Manifesto for the Abolition of Interest Slavery.*" The book explained the highly adverse impact of interest-based debt in general as "slavery" and, in particular, German war debts and their economic consequences that exacerbated the nation's economic impoverishment. He proclaimed interest-bearing debt as the trap that forced the economy to depend on foreign creditors. Feder called it "*the interest slavery.*" He also condemned the financial system as the tool that fed "Mammon." Feder had a strong definition for what interest represented and described it as "*the effortless and endless influx of goods based on the mere ownership of moneywithout any addition of labor.*" Feder often employed mathematical logic in explaining his arguments.

Feder compared the fortunes gained from the operations of interest-rate mechanism with industrial profits as depicted by the graph above. He argued that returns from money-to-money dealings and speculation would increase exponentially with time but never reach an end. The "Rothschild" curve demonstrated the gains from interest rate-based transactions, and the "*Leihkapital,*" or loan capital, which referred to speculative behaviour. Meanwhile, returns from industries, shown by the industrial capital (*Industrie Kapital*) curve, increased gradually reaching a maximum then decayed. Profits from committing to real production was measurable, finite and contingent on the outcome of the workings of the economy. These curves demonstrate the difference between gains from loan capital—that is from transactions employing the interest-rate mechanism or risk transfer—and profits from industrial capital—risk sharing transactions. The latter shows a more natural movement while the Rothschilds' curve showed an autonomous growth infinitely while "*dragging everything with it.*"

Thus, Feder proposed several policy recommendations, all necessary for abolishing interest-rate payment. He urged ignoring the war debt in order to achieve fiscal stability. He further proposed empowering the Reichsbank with more direct control over banks and other financial institutions. The latter approach often referred to "*nationalization*" of the private banking system. However, Feder never demanded nationalization in his writings. What he demanded was a policy that could abrogate the

96   P. SWASTIKA AND A. MIRAKHOR

rule of "*every kind of possession carries an entitlement to earnings*" principle.[22] He explained the economic consequences of such attitude. Such a rule neglected the real value of labour capital, shifted people's focus from creating work to raising money, and forced fiscal policy to become complicated and expensive. Unnecessary inflation occurred as continued interest and compounding brought about immeasurable risks and uncertainty to the aggregate economy. Feder's proposal was critical to stopping this vicious circle and creating an efficient channel for allocation and circulation of financial resources as well provide necessary institutional framework to deter hoarding behaviour.[23]

In the early 1920s, the economy entered a turbulent phase in which the exchange rate of plummeted and the cost of living increased. Then, it was recorded that 1 kg bread cost 428 milliard paper marks; 1 kg butter cost 5600 milliard paper marks, a newspaper cost 200 milliard paper marks, a tram ticket cost 150 milliard paper marks (Bresciani Turroni, 1968, p. 25). After the Treaty of Versailles, in May 1921, Germany signed another agreement with the Allied forces (The London Agreement) on the reparation payment. The Agreement settled on the liability of 132 billion gold marks (about $31.4 billion) with a fixed annual installment amounting to $500 million plus 25% of the total value of the country's exports, around $750 million a year (Scroggs, 1934, p. 520).

Since the Government controlled the monetary authority, it demanded a continuous supply of *mark* from the Reichsbank. The currency exchange rate plunged and the inflation rate climbed throughout 1920–1921. In 1923, the value of the currency exchange rate dropped to an unprecedented historical level. The Reichsmark totally collapsed leading

---

[22] "*Dem Zinsprinzip zuliebe, einer im tiefsten Grunde irrigen staatlichen Vorstellung gemäß, daß jede Art von Besitz Anrecht auf Erträgnis habe, haben wir uns in die Zinsknechtschaft des*" (Feder, 1919, p. 13).

[23] Feder argued that, in the interest-economy, people tended to withdraw money from the market, therefore, the authority issued paper more than the actual market needed for liquidity. "*Indeed, it cannot be denied that our issued paper currency, as much as about 40Bn, is also not in circulation but for the most*" (Feder, 1919, p. 32).

to what became known as *"the hyperinflationperiod."*[24] This period heralded emergence of more serious of macroeconomic problems.

Some conventional economists viewed the continuous budget deficit of the government as the problem causing the deep economic crisis.[25] Others believed the "passive" balance of payments policies—a condition where the import was far larger than revenues from export—had set off the fall of Reichsmark value against foreign currencies. Several economists recognized the faulty monetary policy that allowed unlimited printing of paper money, a drop in gold and foreign reserves, and uncontrolled Government spending to cover war reparations.[26] The nominal value of the currency plummeted to a level where it became worthless. Prices and taxes increased and the population lost confidence in governments. Karl Helfferich, the then prominent German economist and former Secretary of Treasury and Interior, identified the problem of inflation as being due to faulty economic system in his article *"Die Autonomie der Reichsbank"* (April 4, 1922) in which he argued: *"Inflation and the collapse of the exchange rate are children of the same parent... the problem of restoring the circulation is not a technical or banking problem; it is a problem of the equilibrium between the load and the capacity of the German economyfor supporting this load"* (Bresciani Turroni, 1968, p. 46).

It had become obvious to all that reforms had become necessary. As well it was recognized that the first priority was to stabilize the value of the currency. To that end, the authorities had to restore public trust in the currency as well as in government securities in the sense that they

---

[24] In a *New York Times* article on the chaotic situation of Germany's economy, dated August 21, 1922, Dr. Helfferich observed, *"Germany is not suffering from inflation, but from scarcity of money, ... the industry and agriculture had exceptional difficulty this season in obtaining the money needed for the season.* The *London Stock Exchange Gazette* agreed to the observations and added: *"The more money is printed and the lower the mark falls, the more anxious are the people to get rid of their cash and to convert it into real values, or to send it out of the country. Inflation thus creates a scarcity of liquid money in the country itself and abundance abroad"* (**Germany's Currency and the Tight Money**, 1922).

[25] Harold James (1984), *"Foreign observers liked to give an alternative explanation that unfunded government budget deficits, which had only, to a small extent, been produced by external payments, had increased the amount of moneyin circulation and thus started a price rise."*

[26] Ibid., *"The currency instability of the early-1920s made the currency into a politically contentious issue. Most Germans, living from 1914 to 1923 through the most rapid inflationthe world had yet seen, at first believed that their misfortune was the result of Allied demands for reparation payments."*

would come to trust that they were value-bearing (*wertbeständiges*).[27] In August 1922 during Cuno Government, Dr. Karl Helfferich proposed to former Secretary of Treasury and Interior a "*transitional currency*" that upheld the principle of "stable value" (*wertbeständiges*). The principle of stable value determined whether the certificate denoted the worth of what it afforded. Moreover, the paper had to be issued in small denominations so the public could accept it as an alternative means of exchange.

Valorization of the paper entailed a simple mechanism of indexation, that was, to attach the value of the paper with the market worth of a representative commodity, i.e., the rye. However, this feature did not render the paper automatically convertible to the base commodity. Only its value was pegged to the market worth of rye. Valorization was to set up a reliable warranty for the value of the money and to prevent inflation, or deflation, on account of speculators and the low value of the currency against foreign exchange or gold. Feldmann (1997, p. 708) wrote that the idea behind such initiative was to "*win confidence either at home or abroad by the 'free forces of the economy,' the so-called 'economic professions' (wirtschaftliche Berufsstände).*" The Government and the Reichsbank accepted the recommendation to stabilize the value of the mark, which was an alternative war currency based on the index price of rye (*Roggen*), hence the "*Roggenrentemark.*" The currency received much criticism for inflating the prices of agriculture products and burdening other economic sectors.

On November 20, 1923, the Reichsbank substituted the *Roggenrentemark* with the "*Rentenmark.*"[28] The principles of the Rentenmark, however, were analogous to the Roggenmark. Both currencies promoted valuation of the monetary unit based on the real value of products and not on gold and foreign reserves holding. The difference between them was the nature of indexation. Unlike the *Roggenrentenmark*, the *Rentenmark* was based on more than one product of the primary sectors—industrial, transportation, agriculture, and mortgage. Such valuation of the

---

[27] Schacht defined '*stable-value currency*' (wertbeständiges) in his book **"Das Ende der Reparationen"** (*The End of Reparations*) by stating, "*The history of the Reichsbank after the war is an excellent and almost complete picture of the multitudinous and difficult problems of money and currency policy. Foremost among them is the search for a stable standard of currency, i.e. for a standard of value which will constitute an invariable measure for the value of all*" (Schacht, 1932, p. 133).

[28] The legal basis for the *Rentenmark* issuance was the October 15, 1923 Gazette on the establishment of the *Rentenbank*.

monetary unit was distinct compared to the conventional methods as the mark was heavily influenced by external sentiments toward Germany, particularly the problem of war reparations.[29]

The *Roggenrentemark* and the *Rentenmark* were considered "deception" to restore the buying power of the currency because alternative means of payments was not effective against inflationary pressures. While the mark was still the legal tender of the nation, the alternative monetary units represented IOU papers; their worth derived from the productive activities of the private sector. These securities were convertible to *Papiermark*. The *Rentenbank* issued the *Rentenmark* with the obligation to reimburse the paper upon the holder's request in as many marks as represented in its nominal value. The holders were assured by the "constant value clause" (*wertbeständiges*) that also allowed them to convert their *Papiermark* into the *Rentenmark* for its equal value to the gold mark. The option was meant to discourage the hoarding behavior and accelerate the circulation of money in the market.[30] Also, the *Rentenmark* had adjusted the exchange rate that was pegged one-on-one between the mark and the US dollar.[31]

The years 1924–1929 showed a temporary improvement in the economy. Signing the Dawes Plan affected the economy positively. Guillebaud (1939) indicated that the Dawes Plan "*had an immense psychological effect on both in Germanyand abroad.*" In brief, the Plan favored Germany. First, it fixed the annual quotas for the reparation payments. Second, it opened more space for the Reichsbank to control the connection between the Reichsmark and the exchange rate. This empowerment

---

[29] It was important to have sufficient foreign currency reserves to support the value of the mark. However, observers cynically stated in *The Glasgow Herald* ("German Financial Reform," Sept. 17, 1923); "*who will lend to a country whose political future is so undefined, and the extent of whose external burdens is so vague and immense as are those of present-day Germany? Money was only found for Austria when that State was relieved from the obligation of paying reparations for twenty years, and was placed under the care of an impartial external authority.*"

[30] The circulation of legal money increased as much as 1.100–1.200 million marks after the introduction of *Rentenmark* (Bresciani Turroni, 1968).

[31] November 20, 1923, the *Rentenmark* was issued at the rate of 1 trillion *Papiermark*, or 4.2 *Rentenmark* for a dollar (1 trillion paper marks = 1 gold mark = 1 *Rentenmark*; as for the exchange rate: 4.2 gold mark = 4.2 *Rentenmark* = 1 dollar).

helped to establish the Agent-General for Reparations Payments[32] with mandate to ensure a balance between reparation payments, the exchange value of the currency, and stabilizing the economy. This office made a moral argument that Allies should consider the economic ability of Germany before demanding reparations.

Despite its ostensible moral pretentions, the Dawes Plan was a debt-restructuring plan. Auld (1934, pp. 11–12) stated, *"The service of the Dawes loan is a direct and unconditional duty of the Reich, chargeable on all its present and future assets and revenues. For the amounts needed as collateral security, a specific first charge on the gross income from the customs and the taxes on tobacco, beer and sugar and from the net revenue of the German Government from the spirits monopoly."*

The Plan had a number of positive dimensions; it provided the Allies and foreign creditors security of a more stable value of the German currency—thus stabilizing the value of the reparation payments.[33] The Dawes Plan also supplied Germany with foreign aid and capital to help the economy to recover from the devastating impact of hyperinflation. Auld (1934, p. 12) pointed out that, upon the financialization of the Dawes Plan, Germany issued sovereign bonds, *"The German Seven Percent External Loan of 1924,"* in several foreign markets in various currencies (the United States, Great Britain, France, Italy, Switzerland, Holland, Belgium, Sweden, and Germany). This policy helped the revival of the

---

[32] According to Northrop (1938, pp. 30, 31), the Agent General for Reparation Payment was the connecting link between the Board of Directors of the Reichsbank and the foreign nations that claimed the right to watch over the stability of the German currency. This council was set up as a layer of protection of the Allies and foreign creditors to *"his own pecuniary interest by actual interference in the moneyand banking organization of the debtor country."* Under the 1924 Gazette, the Agent General had the right to select the President of the Reichsbank and the members of the Board of Directors, and was required to hold a meeting once a month to discuss matters of general policy. According to Randall Germain (1997, p. 36), the Agent General was *the essential element* of the Dawes Plan since its task laid precisely in the managing decision of transferring reparation payment from Germany to the Allies without jeopardizing the currency value of the German mark.

[33] The Dawes Plan also changed the course of the Reichsbank through The Bank Act of August 30, 1924, with the following purposes: *1. to regulate the circulation of moneythroughout the Reich; 2. to facilitate the clearance of payments; and 3. to provide for the utilization of available capital.* The 1924 Bank Law had also broken the old association of government control and made the institution as a *privately owned stock company controlled by its own Board of Directors* (Northrop, 1938, pp. 28–29).

economy as indicted by several macroeconomic indicators, such as investment, employment, trade and national income. Auld (1934, p. 15) further tied the value of the Dawes Plan to the economy's revival, *"The Dawes loan was the basis of Germany's revival—the foundation stone on which had erected her present robust industrial structure."*

However, opposite views were expressed regarding the Plan's contributions to the economy. Some economists thought the Dawes loan scheme failed to restore stability to the economy as it was perceived as "artificial" recovery which led to emergence of further economic problems. Harold James (1984) unequivocally explained that the economic growth in Germany in the late 1920s depended on foreign borrowing. There were at least three major impacts from the Plan on the economy.

First, the false prosperity concealed the country's actual economic condition. The wrong signal forced Germany to continue servicing reparation payments while neglecting the domestic conditions. Schacht (1934) suggested half of the foreign loans between 1924 and 1930 ($10 billion with an average interest rate of 6%) went to the Allies as reparation payments.[34]

Second, the foreign loans increased Government expenditures through projects that should not have been undertaken. Moreover, such short-term loans were not adequate for funding long-term projects, creating a crisis at maturity. Guillebaud (1939, p. 12) described the situation as *"inevitably disastrous"* when lenders withdrew their funds from the market during the Depression.[35] While creating the illusion of macroeconomic stability, the Dawes Plan adversely affected public welfare, but only to improve the appearance of macroeconomic.

Concerns about the sustainability of the Dawes Plan led to Young Conference in 1929.[36] An agreement was reached on June 7, 1929, in

---

[34] Schacht (1934) continued: *"... out of the $10 billion borrowed, approximately half was used in reparations payments to the victorious governments, while only half remained for investment in Germany"*. In an article published in *The Saturday Review of Literature*, No. 13, Vol. VIII, edition October 31, 1931, Lamont (1931) quoted: *"...Wiggin report points out, that from 1924 to 1930 there was a net influx of capital into Germany of about 18 billion Reichsmarks, and during the same period Germany paid out in reparations over 10 billion Reichsmarks"*.

[35] Another resentment of the Dawes Plan was the interference of foreign lenders and allies in the national monetary policy through The Agent General for Reparation Payment.

[36] The Young Conference, held in Paris in the spring of 1929, was a result of the report by Mr. S. Parker Gilbert, a reparation agent, in June 1929. The report pointed to several

the spirit of the Allied claim that Germany was still obligated to make reparation payments. The Dawes Plan attempted to take into consideration Germany's interests, it ratified the clauses supporting the country's wish to regain control over its currency and other economic affairs.

First, the Plan demanded international supervision and the Agent-General Committee to include experts of German nationality (Northrop, 1938, p. 31). Second, it established the Bank for International Settlements (BIS), a neutral body, for managing international transfer payments to the Allies and foreign creditors. The BIS hoped to eliminate domination of a foreign country. For the Allies, the plan reduced the annuity amount and the total reparation payment. The annuity term was to run for 59 years as follows: RM 1, 988 million a year for the first 37 years, and RM 1, 600 million a year for the following 22 years, and around RM 660 million were to be "*an unconditional and not-postponable demand*" from the German railroads and the Reich's budget out of special taxes, as regulated by the Plan (Northrop, 1938, p. 209).[37]

Both parties, the Allies and Germany were unsatisfied with the Agreement. For the Allies, the Young Plan meant a decrease in the total reparation payments and a "loss" in their financial interest. For the Germans, the Young Plan added a series of adverse economic elements. Because of the persisting debt load, the Government could not launch programs to improve the conditions of the labour market or the people's income. The unemployment rate was high and increasing, while wages

---

economic uncertainties and political upheavals that occurred in the country from to the Dawes Plan. The growing foreign debt for bankers' short-term gain while the growing rate of unemployment caused political unrest, which resulted in the rising vote of the National Socialist German Workers Party and the loss of power of the Republican government. Also, the report indicated that Germany could not further service the reparation debts and proposed the Allied countries and foreign creditors to focus on restoring "*balance trade and the development of long-term capital investments for productive ends*" (Northrop, 1938, p. 201).

[37] The Committee of Experts reported, "*By the final reduction and fixation of the German debt, by the establishment of a progressive scale of annuities, and by the facilities which the new Bank offered for lessening disturbance in the payment of the annuities, it sets the seal of the inclusion of the German debt in the list of international settlements. If it involves appreciable reduction of payments to the creditor countries ... it at the same time eliminates the uncertainties ... and were equally inimical to the interest of the Debtor and to the Creditors, by substituting a definite settlement under which the Debtor knows the exact extent of his obligations*" (Report of the Committee of Experts, pp. 47–48 in Northrop, 1938, p. 209).

5 THE FOUNDATION OF THE GERMAN ECONOMY ... 103

were high and sticky. Germany was still restrained by the terms set by the foreign powers that prevented the Government from serving its people with better economic policy.

THE GERMAN ECONOMY DURING THE GREAT DEPRESSION

The Great Depression was worldwide. The shock of the US stock market crash in October 1929 severely affected the global economy. After the US economy's collapse in May 1931, one of the strongest banks in Europe, the Austrian *Kreditanstalt*, declared bankruptcy. For Germany, the adverse impact from this bank was instantaneous as foreign capital investments were withdrawn from the country. In the second week of June 1931, Germany lost as much as RM 610 millions of gold and currency in the financial markets (Northrop, 1938, p. 214). The domestic market was shocked. The Government announced an emergency decree, cutting much of the social and unemployment insurances and increasing tax rates.

The decision was a blow to domestic demand since public spending sustained most of the consumption at the time. One of the largest textile companies in Germany, the *Nordwolle* of Bremen, collapsed. Soon afterward, on July 13, 1931, the Danat Bank could not open and declared insolvency.[38] On July 14 and 15, 1931, an emergency decree (Article 48 Weimar Constitution) declared "*two days of bank holiday.*" On June 20, 1931, President Hoover announced a one-year moratorium on all intergovernmental debts, including Germany's debt.

The global crisis ignited a spirit of economic reform. In Germany, economists discussed the situation, seeking workable solutions. Also, groups affiliated with political parties, such as the National Socialists (NSDAP) and communists, offered their economic plans to the public. The NSDAP manifesto, for instance, proposed a 25-points program 11 of which focused on the party's financial plan. These plans appealed for canceling war debts, demanding a colony area for Germany, and abolishing interest rate from the financial system.

Another think-tank group not belonging to political powers, the Friedrich List Society, proposed an alternative solution prepared by

---

[38] It was said that the Danat Bank "*had taken too many municipal bills, and its crisis came when it acknowledged this by refusing to renew a loan to the City of Berlin*" (James, 1984, p. 79).

Wilhelm Lautenbach, a prominent scholar and senior adviser to the Economic Ministry. On September 16, 1931, in a closed meeting of the Friedrich List Society, Lautenbach presented a recovery program to reverse the worsening economic conditions. Lautenbach's proposal centers on expanding domestic credit (*heimische Kreditexpansion*). This solution was to stimulate national demand and accelerate capital distribution. A national demand involved "*public or publicly supported works which are essential to the value increase for the economy and would have to be done under normal conditions in any case*" (Cramer, April 18, 2003). Money circulation could be accelerated only in a setting where transaction costs were low. According to Dr. Lautenbach, the elements of transaction costs were interest rate, taxes, and wages. Deciding what constituted reasonable transaction costs was not impossible, considering that taxes and salaries were automatically adjusted if creation of liquidity was inexpensive. In other words, the Reichsbank had to bankroll the Government by ensuring enough liquidity through its open market operation.

This policy would reflect a positive gesture by the central bank to sustain market liquidity while adjusting the rate of credit according to supply and demand in the domestic market. Adjusting credit function would have had contributed to the expansion of production and produced a minimal increase in the rate of monetary expansion equilibrated to the rate of growth and expansion in productive activities. Lautenbach believed that inflation only occurred when credit was larger than that needed by the real sector. Therefore, the solution for avoiding either depression or inflation problems was to balance the demand for new public infrastructures and their financing needs. When credit grew at an "equal" rate with the expansion in production, a rise in output and consumption would be induced without the threat of potential inflation.[39] The essential element of creating a new national demand granted the Reichsbank more authority in managing the financial system for a more active participation of the real sector.

It is also worth noting that during 1932–1933, a monetary experiment emerged in *Wörgl*, a small town in the Austrian Alps. The Plan's

---

[39] Expansion of credit without a commensurate expansion of production posed a potential threat of inflation and had the movement of pricing and wages fail to correspond with such policies because of stickiness. Therefore, Lautenbach also proposed government intervention to wage policy and price cartel of the necessary commodities, which he called "negative measures."

implementation led to such a rapid economic recovery to attract many international tourists to the city who wished to witness its economic miracle. Wörgl became "*the economic Mecca.*" *Stories about* the city and its mayor appeared in various articles in European, American, and Australian newspapers. An article entitled "*Bucking the Bankers,*" written by Harrison Brown, was published in the London "*New Statesman and Nation.*" The article claimed: "*At this moment, in an obscure room in Vienna, ease is being fought which many people around the world are convinced will become historical... The Mayor and Corporation of Wörgl, in the Tyrol, are being tried for having saved their little township from starvation...*" (December 2, 1933).

In another article, dated August 9, 1933, *The World News, NSW*, a Sydney-based newspaper asserted that the magic of the Wörgls monetary experiment has "*become the talk of Central Europe because it has invented its financial system, with the astonishing results*" (Brown, 1934). In addition to journalists, a number of prominent economists scrutinized the financial mechanism adopted by Worgl with keen interest. Irving Fisher, Professor at The Yale University, endorsed the mechanism and commented in his book "*Stamp Script*", "*...(the) extra speed, i.e. the fast circulation of the stamp scrip mechanism, is of the utmost benefit in a depression when everyone is afraid to spend real money...*" (1933).

Wörgl and its mayor, Michael Unterguggenberger, deserved the attention. Their success in repelling the Great Depression within a brief period was an outstanding achievement for any government. Until the spread of the Depression across the region, Wörgl had a railway depot and a cement and cellulose factories. In 1929, because of the economic chaos, the railroad terminal was forced to shut down. By summer 1931, all plants stopped operating, and employees discharged (Brown, 1934).

In the wake of the experiment in 1932–1933, the Wörgl undertook several construction and renovation projects under the relief work program. The list of public projects was exhaustive.[40] Tax revenues increased, and the local government funded the relief work program and

---

[40] Unterguggenberger (1933, p. 62) listed the focus of experiment in 1932, the reconditioning of the main road to the railway station; settling the city's water system; the construction of bridge of Wildschönauerstraße; the relocation of building; the construction of Wildschönauerstraße; the construction of the water reservoir in Winkl; the construction of forest paths and the provision of about 300 seats for that purpose; and repair and gravelling of farm roads. "Projects up to the first quarter of 1933 include the opening access from and to Aubach gorge by constructing a new path and several bridges,

106   P. SWASTIKA AND A. MIRAKHOR

settled its debt. The unemployment rate dropped briskly; "*unemployed had been almost all absorbed*" (*High Finance: A Small Town's Experiment, Spend or Lose*, 1933).

The crisis placed great stress on the conventional monetary system. The Mayor of Worgel, Unterguggenberger, pondered on the crisis that struck the United States which rippled across the world in an article entitled "*Die Geld-Reform von Wörgl*," he wrote: "*Slow circulating moneyhas been the cause of this unprecedented economic crisis and created millions of people in distress. It is the time, through plain recognition and decisive action, to save the industry (i.e. the real economy), so humanity will not plunge into a civil war and confusion*" (*Geld und Albeit Magazine*, Jan–Feb 1933).

He further explained that the weak circulation emerged also because of the interest rate mechanism since the financial surplus holders expected to be rewarded with a sufficiently high enough rate to induce them to part with their money. In other words, they set a minimum on the rate they would accept. During crises borrowers are unwilling to pay that kind of interest. Since the pulse of economic life depended on the volume of exchange of goods and services, the proposed system had to restore economic growth and stability to uplift the morale of the population. The plan to impose a depreciation cost on the cash holdings helped released the economic energies of financial resources to achieve these objectives and reduce the negative power of interest rate mechanism.

On July 8, 1932, the municipality issued the first *Arbeitswertschein* (work-notes). This alternative monetary system fulfilled the principle of stamp money of Gesell, which charged a depreciation cost to cash holdings. To issue the note, the Government had to deposit its Austrian Shillings in the local savings bank, the *Raiffeisen Bank*, which held a 100% cover for the issued amount. The municipality could issue 1800 Austrian Schillings in 1, 5, and 10 Schillings denomination.

The note showed a date and stamp column and announced the loss of 1% of its face value at the close of each month. The value, however, could be kept at its nominal value, by adding a stamp of 1% at the end of the month. If the holder did not spend the note until following month, he could buy the stamp with Austrian Schillings and stick it on the note to preserve its face value. It was also convertible to the Austrian Schillings

---

renovation of the square near the Brook Bridge in Wörgl, the extension of the Silvio-Gesellstraße, the new Friedhofstraße, the Jahnstraße, and adjoining the Jahnstraße with the Salzburgerstraße."

5 THE FOUNDATION OF THE GERMAN ECONOMY ...   107

at the local savings bank, only with 2% discount of their nominal value. This process was controlled by a committee consisting of the mayor, the commandant of the local army, and a member of the city council.

The municipality did not encounter many challenges in distributing the certificate. It persuaded four members of the town council, themselves traders, to accept the tokens in their stores ("Ending Depression: How an Austrian Village Did It," 1933). Soon, other businesses and stores in the city agreed to accept the note. The local government also paid its employees and contractors for the relief works with the note.[41] According to von Muralt (1933), the first issuance was 1800s and rose to around 3000s. At a later period as much as 12,000s notes were issued, and so 12,000s had to be deposited. Besides salary payment, the low-income received the relief note as cash subsidy. The note paid the local government taxes and non-tax charge. That was how the circulated notes returned to the possession of the municipality. Only the payment for Railway and postal business and the Federal taxes had to be paid in Austrian Schillings. Credible sources also indicated that there was a negligible effect of the note issuance to the local inflation rate. One year after its circulation, M. Claude Bourdet observed prices and costs of goods and services did not increase. Alexander von Muralt, an Austrian economist, reached the same conclusion. He noted that small increases in inflation rate were because prices of essential foodstuff in Wörgl were the same as those of Innsbruck and Kitzbühel.

To sum up, practices and economic concepts developed over the period of the nineteenth century to the early 1930s established a compelling case for the adoption of risk sharing principle in Germany's economy. As early as the nineteenth century, the *Wiederlegung*, *Sendegeschäft*, and *Kuxen* contracts appeared to have facilitated trade in Germany. The enactment of the Customs Union and construction of railways nexus between cities also improved exchange transactions and accelerated economic growth. Special case for rail projects, issuing railway notes, was a new instrument that involved the holder of certificates in a given company's affairs. Joint-stock banks offered partnership arrangements that promoted entrepreneurship and creativity in establishing new businesses. In university, the economy was presented as one in which both the individual and

---

[41] The recipients had previously agreed to accept this form of payment.

public were equally important. The Government arranged a system for coordination among market participants.

In the twentieth century, resentments arose against the interest rate-based financial system. While the rentier class dominated the global economy, scholars lamented the inherent problems of the interest rate-based system. Silvio Gesell criticized the monetary system based on interest rate. He argued that positive returns on money-to-money transaction prevent a healthy circulation of capital allowing speculators and hoarders to enter the financial market and create obstacles for economic progress. He proposed a surcharge, *Zahlungsakte* (money stamp), at an annual fee of 5%. The call for rejecting domination of the conventional system lasted throughout the 1920s.

In the wake of the WWI defeat, population's anger toward economic injustice, represented by Germany's war debt imposed by the Allies as reparation, was intensifying. Gottfried Feder, one of the founders of National Socialism, wrote a small essay commenting on the situation. He called the Government to dare *to break the interest thralldom* and refuse to agree on war reparations based on social justice and people's welfare. In his book, Feder presented data from the working of the German monetary economy. He showed the progressively larger growth of gains from the rent on money as compared with a more natural and orderly growth of profit from real sector economic activities. He showed the startling difference between the growth of earning differences between what he called "loan capital", meaning the earnings from debt-creating flows, and "industrial capital", meaning capital mobilized from selling shares. He argued that the former was a serious drag on the economy, caused impoverishment and "interest slavery" that tended to "*drag everything with it.*"

Unlike in the nineteenth century, there was little evidence for risk sharing in the first quarter of the twentieth century. However, these periods marked another milestone in the concept of finance for the non-interest-rate monetary system. Criticism of interest rate-based system grew markedly, not on the ground of Divine commandment, but from the perspective of real socio-economic injustice. Gesell and Feder were the icons of the campaign against interest rate in Germany. Gesell's concept on the surcharge for hoarders was applied in the city of Wörgl. The so-called depreciating money circulated in tandem with the Austrian Schilling for payments without incurring problems of inflation. Tax revenue increased, which allowed the city to undertake beautification projects. With increasing employment and income, town people enjoyed an improvement in their wellbeing.

There are two important points to make. First, in a risk sharing financial system, joint-stock banks promoted social and economic wellbeing. They collected financial resources from selling retail shares and extended financing by assuming a portion of ownership of the client company.[42] Financial resources become capital when converted to machinery and equipment. Moreover, attempts were made to improving coordination among market participants in order to reduce transaction costs and spur exchange and trade activities. That was why partnership contracts, customs union, railway constructions, and joint-stock banks, contributed to helping Germany to become an industrial nation in the nineteenth century. Second, events of the early twentieth century in the city of Wörgl showed a vision of removing interest rate from the financial system. Charging hoarding costs made lending and borrowing costly. Consequently, the system induced rapid circulation of idle cash and a dynamic exchange of goods and services. Even the size of tax payments to the city increased. Reducing the power of the interest rate mechanism had reduced transaction cost. In an economic system without the interest-rate mechanism and applied risk sharing, as proposed by Islamic finance, transaction costs became low or non-existent, and the allocation of financial resources more efficient.

These theories and practices suggested two principles that were institutionalized in the market. Germany had expanded its economy by mobilizing resources from the people and investing in public investment projects. This first institution was implemented well before the nineteenth century. The principle had set the maintenance of social welfare profoundly ahead of personal economic motives. Therefore, every society member had to be rule-compliant, and the State enforced the rules.

The second institution was the government's focus on value creation. By "value" we mean the returns the society gained from economic policy implementation. This principle was observed in the construction of the Saxony Railway, the Customs Unions implementing the theory of Gesell and Feder, the proposal of Lautenbach to end the depression, and the Wörgl miracle. The campaign against the interest rate-based debt system argued that an optimal aggregate return could be achieved if money

---

[42] This structure was familiar in Islamic finance called "*two-tier modaraba*" (silent-partnership).

110 P. SWASTIKA AND A. MIRAKHOR

circulated with a volume needed to buy the output that the real sector produced. The focus was on providing the liquidity needed by projects that focused on improving infrastructure and welfare. This proposal had inspired Mayor Unterguggenberger of Wörgl to implement a stamp script and non-interest rate policy.

REFERENCES

Auld, G. P. (1934). The Dawes and Young loans: Then and now. *Foreign Affairs, 13*(1), 6–25.

Braudel, F. (1982). *Civilization and capitalism, 15th–18th century*. University of California Press.

Bresciani Turroni, C. (1968). *The economics of inflation*. John Dickens & Co. Ltd.

Brown, H. (1934, March). Saved township from starvation: Countless community credit, novel Austrian experiment that met a crucial position. *Nambour Chronicle and North Coast Advertiser*, p. 12.

Cameron, R. E. (1953). The credit mobilier and the economic development of Europe. *The Journal of Political Economy, LXI*(6), 461–488.

Connolly, D. E. (2005). *Problems of Textual Transmission in Early German Books on Mining: 'Der Ursprung Gemeybber Berckrecht' and the Norwegian*. Bergkornung: The Ohio State University.

Cramer, C. (2003). Does inequality cause conflict? *Journal International Development, 15*, 397–412. https://doi.org/10.1002/jid.992.

Da Rin, M. (1997). Finance and technology in early industrial economies: The role of economic integration. *Research in Economics, 51*, 171–200.

de Lara, Y. G. (2003). Commercial partnerships. In *Oxford encyclopaedia of economic history* (pp. 480–483). Oxford University Press.

Feder, G. (1919). *Das Manifest zur Brechung der Zinsknechtschaft des Geldes*. Muenchen: Verlag Jos.C.Huber.

Feldman, G. D. (1997). *The great disorder: Politics, economics, and society in the German inflation, 1914–1924*. New York, NY: Oxford University Press, Inc.

Fisher, I. (1932). *Booms and depressions: Some first principles*. Adelphi Company.

Fisher, I. (1933). *Stamp scrip*. Adelphi Company.

Forrester, R. E. (2006). *The general steam navigation company c.1850–1913: A business history*. Dissertation, University of Greenwich.

Garvy, G. (1975). Keynes and the economic activists of pre-Hitler Germany. *The Journal of Political Economy, 83*(2), 391–405.

Germain, R. D. (1997). *States and global finance in the world economy*. Cambridge University Press.

5 THE FOUNDATION OF THE GERMAN ECONOMY ... 111

Greif, A. (2006). *Institutions and the path to the modern economy: Lessons from medieval trade* (pp. 1–31). Cambridge University Press.

Guillebaud, C. W. (1939). *The economic recovery of Germany from 1933 to the incorporation of Austria in March 1938.* Macmillan.

Helfferich. (1922). Germany's currency and the tight money. *New York Times,* 21 August 1922.

James, H. (1984). The causes of the German banking crisis of 1931. *The Economic History Review, 37*(1), 68–87.

Kensinger, J. W., & Poe, S. L. (2005). Corporate ownership is not always the best policy. In A. H. Chen (Ed.), *Research in finance.* Research in Finance (Vol. 22, pp. 1–31). Emerald Group. https://doi.org/10.1016/S0196-3821(05)22001-4.

Keynes, J. M. (1936). *The general theory of employment, interest, and money.* London: Macmillan.

Lamont, T. W. (1931, October 31). *Reparations and war debts.* The Saturday Review of Literature, Vol. VIII, No.13.

Lindberg, E. (2008). The rise of Hamburg as a global marketplace in the seventeenth century: A comparative political economy perspective. *Comparative Studies in Society and History, 50*(3), 641–662.

List, F. (1833). *Über ein sächsisches Eisenbahnsystem als Grundlage eines allgemeinen deutschen Eisenbahnsystems.* Leipzig: A.G. Liebeskind.

List, F. (1885). *The national system of political economy.* History of Economic Thought Books. Longmans, Green & Co.

Northrop, M. B. (1938). *Control policies of the Reichsbank 1924–1933.* Columbia University.

Postan, M. M. (1973). *Medieval trade and finance.* Cambridge University Press.

Punt, H. M. (2010). *Het Vennootschapsrecht Van Holland, Zeeland En West-Friesland In De Rechtspraak Van De Hoge Raad Van Holland, Zeeland En West-Friesland.* Dissertation Universiteit Leiden, Netherland.

Riesser, J. (1911). *The great German banks and their concentration.* Government Printing Office National Monetary Commission.

Sayous, A. (1936). The bourgeoisie of Geneva in the age of the reformation. *The Economic History Review, 6*(2), 194–200.

Schacht, H. (1932). *Das Ende Der Reparationen.* Oldenburg: Gerhard Stalling A.G.

Schacht, H. (1934, June 17). The German viewpoint. *The New York Times.*

Scroggs, W. O. (1934). *German debts and export bounties.* Council on Foreign Relations, Inc.

Tribe, K. (1995). *Strategies of economic order: German economic discourse, 1750–1950.* Ideas in context. Cambridge University Press. https://doi.org/10.1017/CBO9780511551529.

Unterguggenberger, M. (1933). The end results of the Woergl experiment. *Annals of Public and Cooperative Economics, 10*(1), 60–63.

Von Muralt, A. (1933). The Woergl experiment with depreciating money. In O. Spann (Ed.), *Ständisches Leben: Blätter für Organische Gesellschafts und Wirtschaftslehre* (Vol. 6). Erneurungs-Verlag.

Whale, P. B. (1930). *Joint stock banking in Germany: A study of the German creditbanks before and after the war*. Routledge.

Wubs-Mrozewicz, J. (2013). *The Hanse in late medieval and early modern Europe: An introduction*. Brill.

Zander, W. (1933). Railway money and unemployment. *Annals of Collective Economy, IX*(3), 355–368.

CHAPTER 6

Risk Sharing Macroeconomic Policies

This chapter presents important dimensions of Germany's macroeconomic policy during the first three years of the Third Reich and analyzes its underlying principles. The reason for the choice of this timeframe is that policies implemented during this period allowed the German economy to recover from its deep depression at a startling rate as unemployment declined significantly to permit the resumption of high rate of economic growth. Moreover, these results were crucial in empowerment of National Socialism. People's trust gained through these policies was exploited for the Party's political agenda. In the wake of this superb economic performance during 1933–1935, Hitler's power, as the leader of National Socialism grew strongly during this period. In the event, unfortunately, his obsession with power trumped Germany's concern with economic progress and society's welfare. The chapter focuses on the economic policies that spurred the creation of jobs and public welfare and contends that a major contributor to these results was the significant reduction of the power of the interest-rate mechanism and creation of risk sharing institutions in the economy. Therefore, the chapter will discuss tenets and modus operandi of the main economic policies that contributed to the revival of the economy.

© The Author(s), under exclusive license to Springer Nature Switzerland AG 2021
P. Swastika and A. Mirakhor, *Applying Risk-Sharing Finance for Economic Development*, Political Economy of Islam, https://doi.org/10.1007/978-3-030-82642-0_6

113

114   P. SWASTIKA AND A. MIRAKHOR

General Conditions: 1932 to January 1933

Economic conditions had worsened considerably by the closing month of 1932;over six million people was unemployed, national income per capita was the lowest since the hyperinflation period of 1924, manufacturers were shutting down for lack of capital, consumer demand, even for necessities, had collapsed due to significant reduction in the income of the households. Following international pressure for a balanced budget, Chancellor Heinrich Brüning rejected several times proposals for fiscal expansion.[1] Hence, the government did not have sufficient resources to stimulate the economy.[2]

Table 6.1 shows that the economy had been moving toward a recession since 1929. The rise in unemployment, the decrease in the national income and productivity led to an economic slowdown and signaled much worse crises on the horizon. Exports declined, and foreign reserves plummeted rapidly. The system failed to attract and sustain foreign capital. Guillebaud (1939) argued capital flight resulted from the perceived uncertainty by foreign investors. The National Socialist and the Communist parties won the 1930 legislative election. The collapse of Austrian *Kreditanstalt* on May 1931 further distressed foreign investors and increased pressures on the monetary system.[3] The memory of the 1923–1924

---

[1] The Government undertook a deflationary policy. It attempted to reduce the operational budget by reshaping their organizations and laying off staff. The remaining officials received reduced salaries by 6% (1930), then, by 1931, up to the total of 21%. The Government also increased taxes on wages from 1 to 5%, and other taxes such as sugar and profit. Unemployed insurance was cut off; wages, rents, and interest rates were also reduced. These measures lowered the living cost, but stressed the crisis condition. As a result, the government increased expenditure on unemployment relief (or *Erwerbslosenfürsorge*) from 1.8 billion RM in 1929 to 2.7 billion in 1930 and to 3.2 billion in 1931. This policy was summed in Brüning's "Emergency Decree".

[2] Guillebaud (1939, p. 30), Schmidt (1934, p. 57), stated that the lowest level of general industrial and economic activity was reached in August 1932, but without the monthly or quarterly statistical data to support the argument. Guillebaud (1939, p. 30, ft. 1) pointed to the similarities in the country's condition in 1919 and 1932, *"the factories were idle, the streets full of beggars; and unemployment, poverty and decline everywhere apparent."*.

[3] Guillebaud (1939, pp. 20–21) stated that in September 1930, the Reichsbank lost 700 million RM in gold and foreign reserves. From end-May to the mid-July 1931, the Reichsbank lost nearly 2 billion RM in gold and foreign exchange. Despite the Hoover moratorium, capital withdrawals continued. By summer 1931, reserves dwindled to less than 1 billion RM.

Table 6.1 Economic data (in annual figure)

Year	GDP per capita (1990 GK$)[a]	Industrial Production Index (1923 = 100)[a]	Unemployment('000 people)[a]	Unemployment Rate (%)[b]	Trade[a] (Mil RM) Export	Trade[a] (Mil RM) Import	Gold and foreign reserves (Mil RM)[c]
1926	3605	78	2010	—	10.7	9.9	2795
1927	3941	98	1327	—	11.1	14.1	2337
1928	4090	100	1391	6.7	12.6	13.9	3257
1929	4051	100	1899	9	13.6	13.7	3095
1930	3973	87	3076	14.6	12.2	10.6	2980
1931	3652	70	4520	22.3	9.7	7.0	1292
1932	3362	58	5575	28.1	5.8	4.8	1059
1933	3556	66	4804	24.4	5.0	4.3	661

[a]Deutsche Bundesbank (2005)
[b]Hetzel (2002, p. 19)

hyperinflation evoked market panic. In the face of the collapsing economy, adjustments and reform policies for stabilization and growth of the economy were much needed.

Before resigning in May 1932, the Brüning Cabinet launched the work-creation program. It was a limited-budget program of 165 million Reichsmark, divided for road works, water works, and job creation. Chancellor Brüning had to approve this reflationary policy because of public pressures. The plan was executed under the government of von Papen, who entered the office in the same month. In June 1932, the Parliament decreed the job creation policy to improve the economic situation. During summer of 1932, von Papen carried out a set of public infrastructure programs, such as housing, land improvement, and capital expenditure as well as railways and the post office. In September, the Government increased the budget for work creation to strengthen the labor market. The plan covered *"incentives for private employers to hire workers and de-emphasized direct government employment."* The budget allocation for these projects increased to 182 million RM (Feinstein et al., 2008, p. 132).

In December 1932, General Kurt von Schleicher replaced von Papen as Chancellor of the Weimar Republic. His term was brief, so he continued the programs of his predecessor. The Commission for Work Creation, a body that focused on organizing the work-creation program, was established—a serious Government gesture for strengthening labor market and the economy. On January 28, 1933, the Commission launched the third job creation part, the *"Sofort"* program, and allocated 500 million RM for its financing, the massive project never commenced during the short-lived Weimar Government. However, it was a valuable "capital" that the National Socialist Government leveraged. As shown in Table 6.2, there was no improvement in the labor market during the chancellorship of von Papen and von Schleicher from 1932 to January 1933.

This dire economic condition provided the National Socialist the competitive edge. The Party pledged to resolve the socio-economic problems. Its top leaders used people's resentments toward failed policies as the main propaganda vehicle to gain votes. Before 1933, the Party had published their *"Twenty-Five Point Program"* for enhancing the welfare of the farmers and the middle-income class. The programs lauded the spirit of leaderships that placed the State's order at the center of activities

Table 6.2
Unemployment statistics (January 1932–January 1933)

1932	Unemployed	Percent unemployed
January	6,014,010	33.23
February	6,128,429	33.94
March	6,034,100	33.51
April	5,739,070	31.41
May	5,582,620	30.46
June	5,475,778	30.00
July	5,392,248	29.71
August	5,223,810	29.06
September	5,102,750	28.45
October	5,109,173	28.35
November	5,355,420	29.66
December	5,772,984	30.78
1933		
January	6,013,612	34.36

Source Guillebaud (1939)

to ensure prosperity for the people. National Socialists intended to reinstall the sovereignty of the Government as they rejected the domination of the economy by foreign powers that forced the Government to act against people's interests.

MACROECONOMIC POLICIES OF THE THIRD REICH: 1933–1935

Between 1933 and 1935, the Third Reich focused on creating millions of jobs. Unemployment was the country's top problem. By end-1932, the number of jobless people reached its peak at 6 million—a grave signal of the country's poor economic performance. The work-creation programs originated in the earlier regime, was relaunched with vigor and on a much larger scale. After his appointment, in his first radio broadcast, Hitler pledged to the German people to resolve the unemployment problem in four years (Hitler, "*Aufruf an das Deutsche Volk!*", 1933a). To that end, the regime maintained and strengthened the policies of work-creation programs inherited from the earlier regime with a stronger pump-priming policy and adoption of ways and means to counter the potential effects of inflation.

118   P. SWASTIKA AND A. MIRAKHOR

This attempt was first formalized under the law against unemployment (*Das Gesetz gegen Arbeitslosigkeit*), launched on June 2, 1933. Six articles were published in the Gazette: The first one, provided 1 billion RM to the Minister of Finance for promoting the national work-creation program. The amount was to be disbursed according to the "Labour Treasury" bills (*Arbeitsschatzanweisungen*) chiefly for renovation, repair and maintenance of public buildings and residence, agricultural and suburban area development, river, water resource, public utility management, and direct subsidy for the economically less-able segment of the population.

The second specified the conditions governing projects to be supported as: (i) the project had to be "*economically valuable*;" (ii) resources were to be provided with assistance if the owner could not undertake the projects due to lack of financial resources[4]; and (iii) labor was to be given priority over capital. The paragraph also strictly restricted importing labor to induce hiring from the domestic labor market.

Three, the law directed the Government to provide social security to the unemployed and the economically less-able class. For an unemployed person, Government provided unemployment insurance, allowance of 25 RM per month (disbursed in "*Bedarfsdeckungsscheine*" or demand certificates) and one daily hot meal for the work bearer (*Träger der Arbeit*), substitutable for cash. For the poor segment of the population, the Government provided demand certificates for purchasing clothing and household necessities at the appointed stores and the local welfare organizations that distributed the requested items. The nominal amount of proper vouchers provided an additional RM 70 million budget for the RM one billion work-creation program (Grebler, 1937, p. 333).

Four, besides the "Labour Treasury bills" (*Arbeitsschatzanweisungen*), the law designated another source of funding for the programs. With more public works ordered by the Ministry of Labour, the financing could be borrowed from the tax revenue.

Five, the law outlined a redemption schedule and allocated part of the labor Treasury bills (*Arbeitsschatzanweisungen*). As it was detailed, the

---

[4] "*Es dürfen nur solche Arbeiten gefördert werden, die volkswirtschaftlich wertvoll sind und die der Eigentümer aus eigener finanzieller Kraft in absehbarer Zeit nicht würde ausführen können.*" (Vossische Zeitung, 1933) (Only work may be promoted that is economically valuable and that the owner would be unable to carry out from his own financial capacity in the foreseeable future.).

Ministry of Finance was to allocate 20% of the budget in every fiscal year, beginning 1934 and continuing to 1938 for redemption payment.

Six, while the percentage was stipulated, the law ordered the Ministry of Finance to designate a special fund for minimal redemption (or *Tilgungsstock*) to assure the availability of the fund.[5]

The national work-creation programs also welcomed cash donations from the coupon rates (the interest rate) to be transferred to Labour Treasury bills and the provision for redemption.[6] In return, volunteers could claim the donated amount as income tax deduction (tax write off) or give the donation receipt to others.[7] The latter provided the higher-income class incentives to participate in the financing of the programs actively.[8] This work-creation program was also known as the Reinhardt plan.

---

[5] The minimum redemption fund was supplied from the collection of grants of the State- and local-government and other public entities, and voluntary donation from the revenue of government's interest-bearing lending.

[6] "*Die Freiwillige Spende zur Förderung der nationalen Arbeit kann geleistet werden durch: 1.Zahlung an ein Finanzamt, Hauptzollamt oder Zollamt; 2. Hingabe von Schatzanweisungen oder Schuldverschreibungen des Deutschen Reiches, der deutschen Länder, Gemeinden und Gemeindeverbände. Mit Schuldverschreibungen sind Zins- und Erneuerungsscheine hinzugaben. Mit der Hingabe gehen die Schatzanweisungen und Schuldverschreibungen (nebst Zins- und Erneuerungsscheinen) in das Eigentum des Arbeitschatzanweisung-Tilgungsstocks über; 3. Abtretung von Forderungen, die in das Schuldbuch des Deutschen Reichs, eines deutschen Landes, einer deutschen Gemeinde oder eines deutschen Gemeindeverbandes eingetragen sind. Die Abtretung ist zugunsten des Arbeitsschatzanweisungs-Tilgungsstocks zu erklären*" (Vossische Zeitung, 1933).

("*The voluntary donation for the promotion of national work can be made by: 1. Payment to a financial office, main customs office or customs office 2. Surrendering treasury notes or debts of the German Reich, the German lands, municipalities and municipal associations. With this surrender, the redeeming certificates, treasury notes and bonds (together with interest and renewal certificates) become part of the eradication and repayment sum to the treasury. 3. assignment of claims placed in the debt register of the German Reich, German country, German municipality or German municipal council, and the assignment is to be declared in favour of the repayment of the treasury (Vossische Zeitung, 1933)).*

[7] The donated amount could be used to deduct either income tax, corporation tax, property tax, or taxes on sales.

[8] Apart from the work-creation programs was the marriage loan. Marriage loan was a non-interest lending given to new wedding couples to encourage marriage, aiming to increase population after the War. The mechanism for the loan was simple. New couple might apply for up to one thousand Reichsmark loan before marriage, but the amount could only be disbursed after marriage. The repayment was to be made on date ten of every month, and amount of installment was as low as one percent of the total loan. For each child of the marriage born, the couple received 25% remittance of the loan. But there was one condition for the application that the woman was a current worker and had been working for a stipulated duration. Accordingly, the government had disbursed

On February 1, 1933, Hitler described the philosophy behind this expansionary policy to the Reichstag as "*capital serves the economy, and the economy serves the Volk.*"[9] The mechanism ensured liquidity by extending credit under the discounting commercial bills mechanism. Project undertakers issued these commercial bills without increasing the risk of business as they were re-discountable at the Central Bank. The Central Bank held the bills because the certificate could be a reserve cover for the currency at a lower price compared to external loans and gold reserves. This mechanism allowed the central government and the municipalities to contract with suppliers and developers without first making cash payments. Bresciani Turroni described this financing arrangement as "*saving-anticipation borrowing*" because investments were undertaken "*before a corresponding amount of savings in moneyform was available*" (1938, p. 83). Therefore, the whole financing system was called "Pre-financing (*Vorfinanzierung*)".

The Reich did not assume sole liability for expenditure arising from the program. Out of 5 billion RM of the projects' cost, about 40% of the expenses were borne by the bearer of pre-financing (or *die Träger der Vorfinanzierung*). They were Die Deutsche Gesellschaft für Öffentliche Arbeiten A.G.; Die Deutsche Bau- und Bodenbank A.G.; Die Deutsche Rentenbank-Kreditanstalt; Die Deutsche Boden-Kultur A.G.; Die Deutsche Siedlungsbank; Die Deutsche Verkehrs-Kredit Bank A.G.; and Volks-und-Staatswirtschaftliche. The principals or the "work-bearers" (*Träger der Arbeit*) were any entity who "*wished to have work carried out under the programs*," [10]including local contractors that carried out reconstruction or renovation of municipal buildings. The Government paid the remaining 60% in the form of direct cash, short-term bills, or financial instruments such as tax-vouchers. It also paid subsidies for homeowners who repaired their dwellings (Schiller, 1936). By end-1935, the expenditure for dwellings repair was up to 2.8 billion RM, out of which 700 million marks were the Government subsidies, an additional

---

523.000 loans or a total sum of 300 million Reichsmark at the end of 1935 (Grebler, 1937, p. 334).

[9] The Speech of Hitler to the Reichstag in March 23, 1933. Hitler, *EntgegennahmeeinerErklärung der Reichsregierung,* 1933 (Acceptance of a Declaration by the Reich Government, 1933) Source: http://www.reichstagsprotokolle.de/Blatt2_w8_bsb 00000141_00036.html.

[10] This definition was introduced by Grebler, in a report prepared for International Labour Conference, entitled: *Work-Creation Policy I,* 1937, p. 345.

2.1 billion RM was house-owners' contribution.[11] The contribution was classified under direct participation because additional investment came from unused funds of the private sector.

The Third Reich started another expansionary project, the motorization plan or "*Motorisierungspolitik*."[12] This project involved two industries, motorcars, and the construction of highways, to run concurrently. Constructing toll-turnpikes and road systems promoted the work-creation program since it was labor-intensive and absorbed the unemployed. The car industry also supported the work-creation. There were two ways in which objectives of this program were fulfilled. First, renovation or road construction system absorbed a high number of labor in a brief period of time.[13] Second, as many historians suggest, the National Socialist Party's high-ranking officials shared special interests in cars and motor projects. Scholars have remarked that Hitler had been greatly interested in motor vehicles and their role in reviving Germany's dignity (Overy, 1975, p. 469). Producing automobiles was seen as an effective way by which German self-confidence and pride would be restored. In turn this restoration would have positive impact on the psychology, innovative ability, and the productive power of German people. Hence, the motorization program was placed at the forefront of the work-creation program.

The Gazette of 27 June 1933 was the legal base for the program by the formation of the National Motor Roads Company (*Reichsautobahnenbedarf GmbH* or RAB) to manage and establish the motor roads system in Germany, including toll and road construction, and reviving the national automobile industry. The National Motor Roads Company closely collaborated with the Ministry of Transportation (*Reichsverkehrsminister*) and as a "subsidiary" under the supervision of the German Railway Company

---

[11] This was under the scheme of the Second Reinhardt Program. Details on the program are explained in later discussion.

[12] One of the items on motorization plan was the roads construction. Numerous studies have concluded that the Weimar Republic started the road construction earlier than the Third Reich. The Weimar government constructed Cologne-Bonn toll (*Autobahnstrecke*) and was open for traffic in August 1932. The regime also initiated a large scale toll-ways from Hannover to Frankfurt am Main and to Basel (HAFRABA line), but never succeeded to complete it due to financing problem.

[13] The construction projects of roads, canals, and bridges (or *Tiefbau*) had already taken place since the late 1932. However, the project *Autobahn* was only launched under the Third Reich.

122   P. SWASTIKA AND A. MIRAKHOR

Table 6.3 Financing work-creation programs

Program	Work creation bills (Mil. RM)	Own resources, credits, etc. (Mil. RM)
National Railways	860	131
National Post Office	77	34
National Motor Roads	300	50

Source Grebler (1937, p. 348)

(the *Reichsbahn*). The Company constructed 6900 km of roads nationwide, from which 3460 km were ready for construction. At the end of 1935, 1808 km were under construction, and 112 km were open to traffic (Grebler, 1937, p. 334). RAB received both financial support and human resources from the parent company.[14]

The financing structure of the "*Motorisierung*" program consisted of a mixture of fiscal and monetary instruments as well as the participation of private initiatives. The planning activities was financed through donations from enterprises under the GEZUVOR (*Gesellschaft zur Vorbereitung der Reichsautobahnen E.V.*). The Government provided several fiscal incentives to the public to stimulate demand for cars. First, they exempted motor taxes for the newly licensed private cars and motorcycles, under the *Reichsgesetzblatt* No. 37 of 10 April 1933. Second, the owners of older cars could compound the annual tax into a lump-sum payment, under the Gazette of 31 May 1933 (*GesetzüberAblösung der Kraftfahrzeugsteuer*). As the result of the latter incentives, by early 1934, the Government received 55 million marks of the compounded tax-payment. The monetary policy, on the other hand, enabled a stable payment system where certificates of RAB were accepted at the *Verkehrskredit Bank* for discounting purposes. The system ensured regular payment to suppliers and contractors amid budget uncertainty of the Government.

Table 6.3 shows the amount collected for Railways, motor roads, and Post Office construction programs by the end of 1935.

---

[14] As for initial capital, RAB received 50 million Reichsmark from the Reichsbahn. This 50 million Reichsmark was later converted to non-interest bearing loan to the parent company in 1938.

6 RISK SHARING MACROECONOMIC POLICIES   123

In addition to direct spending and the bills, the Reich applied fiscal measures, such as tax remission certificates, to finance projects. The remission certificate connected the pay-offs for the projects to the Government receipt *ahead of single fiscal years.*

As for the programs, the decisive breakthrough for the battle against unemployment under the NSDAP regime materialized through the "First Reinhardt Program." The provision for the program was based on the Law on the Reduction of Unemployment (*Das Gesetz zur Verminderung der Arbeitslosigkeit*) of June 2, 1933. The Government allocated 1 billion RM for financing the work-creation bills for various projects, such as housing, agricultural and suburban settlement, river regulation, public utilities, and roads construction. In principle, the law stipulated financing for economically valuable projects—those with potential to create additional employment projects and are thus economically useful to the society (*volkswirtschaftlichwertvoll*) but which could not be under taken or suspended by the owners due to their inability to mobilize financing.[15]

Furthermore, on June 27, 1933, the Reichstag passed the law on the establishment of "*Reichsautobahnen*" organization, "*Das Gesetzüber die Errichtungeines Unternehmens Reichsautobahnen*" which undertook the building of 7000 km of *Autobahn* (turnpike) under budget allocation of 3.5 billion RM. On September 21, 1933, the "*Zweite Gesetz zur Verminderung der Arbeitslosigkeit*" instituted the distribution of 500 million RM for the "Second Reinhardt Program." The budget of the Reich funded this program as a subsidy for house-owners to repair, renovate, or reconstruct their dwellings, under the stipulated terms and condition.[16] Also, between July and November 1933, decrees such as: The Reich Hereditary Farm Act "*Reichserbhofgesetz*;" The Reich Agricultural Estate "*Reichsnährstand*;" The Measures for the Market and Price Regulation of

---

[15] *Nur diedarlehenweise Verausgabung sollte geschehen zur Förderung solcher Arbeiten, "die volkswirtschaftlich wertvoll sind und die der Träger der Arbeit in absehbarer Zeit nicht würde ausführen können."* (The only loan to disburse should be to promote such work "which are of economic value and which the worker cannot fulfil in the foreseeable future").

[16] The subsidy was granted to house-owners who "*spent from two to four times the amount of the subsidy out of his own or borrowed resources* " (Guillebaud, 1939, p. 40). The Reich also allocated 360 million Reichsmarks for interest-subsidy for the home-owners who borrowed money to spend on the construction, in the amount of 4% of the borrowed money for six years (to be redeemed by the Reich between 1934 and 1939) (Schiller, 1936, p. 56).

124   P. SWASTIKA AND A. MIRAKHOR

Agricultural Products; The Act of the Creation of a New German Peasantry; and The Act for the Formation of Compulsory Cartels were passed as the legal basis for the Government's aggressive action to provide jobs for everyone. These measures laid the necessary foundation for recovery based on investment and the creation of jobs rather than direct transfers to consumers.[17]

To appreciate the intensiveness of the programs, Table 6.4 lists the work-creation projects and the allocation and the disbursed amount for the realization of the projects up to December 1934.

WORK-CREATION BILLS
(ARBEITBESCHAFFUNGSWECHSELN)

The work-creation bills were crucial instrument for the success of the policies to revive the economy. These Bills enabled the funding of massive public projects without imposing huge financial burdens on the Reich's finances. This initiative has evoked many claims, particularly from some historians who have asserted that the work-creation bills were a trick to expand the state-controlled economy. Wolfe, one of these historians, wrote: "*The monetary device used by the Nazis to deal with the unemployment crisis, the famous 'work-creation Bill,' was a sort of practical financial joke played on the German credit system.*" (Wolfe, 1955, p. 393).

It is further argued that bills shifted the burden of financing of work-creation projects to the Reichsbank. They often referred to the statistics that showed that, by end-1934, more than half of the circulated bills were held at the Reichsbank (see Table 6.5).[18] The Reichsbank held about 60% of the bills through the second semester of 1934. Although apparently convincing, the Table also demonstrates the decreasing trend in the number of work-creation bills held at the Reichsbank over 1935 and going forward, thereby rendering the claim seem erroneous. Under

---

[17] "*They have proceeded along the common-sense lines that work and production alone constitute the real source of the wealth of a community, and have relegated moneyto the subordinate though very important role of financing investmentin all its forms, including output of every kind -but chiefly output in the production goods industries; and they have left it to the investmentand employment thus created to produce incomes and savings*" (Guillebaud, 1939, p. 214).

[18] Schiller (1936, p. 132) stated slightly different data. According to Schiller, two thirds of 2600 million Reichsmark of the circulated bills were discounted at the Reichsbank and one third of the bills were absorbed by the banks (as liquid asset) and in the market.

Table 6.4 Estimated & approved plan of work creation program

Program	The allocated fund			The approved and executed fund			
	Pre-financing	Budget	Total	Approved until		Paid until	
				31 Dec 1933	31 Dec 1934	31 Dec 1933	31 Dec 1934
A. The Government Measures							
1. Papen-Program	288.0	—	288.0	286.5	287.5	236.1	282.5
2. Sofort-Program	600.0	—	600.0	559.4	597.7	350.3	559.5
3. The First Reinhardt	1000.0	—	1000.0	678.8	949.6	65.4	694.5
Total I	1888.0	—	1888.0	1524.7	1834.8	651.8	1536.5
II. 4. Suburban Settlement	—	83.0	83.0	75.0	80.8	67.2	78.6
5. Housing Repair Grants (March 1932–Jan 1933)	—	102.0	102.0	102.0	102.0	102.0	102.0
6. The Government Building Loans for House Construction (Sept. 32)		20.0	20.0	18.2	20.1	3.7	17.0
7. Bedarfsdeckungscheine		70.0	70.0	70.0	70.0	30.0	70.0
8. The Second Reinhardt Program							

(continued)

Table 6.4 (continued)

Program	The allocated fund			The approved and executed fund			
				Approved until		Paid until	
	Pre-financing	Budget	Total	31 Dec 1933	31 Dec 1934	31 Dec 1933	31 Dec 1934
a) Financing from Capital	—	500.0	500.0	400.0	499.4	—	410.0
b) Receipts from Interest	—	360.0	360.0		360.0	—	50.0
Total II	—	1135.0	1135.0	665.2	1132.3	202.9	727.6
Total A. (I + H)	1888.0	1135.0	3023.0	2189.9	2967.1	854.7	2264.1
B. Other Corporate Measures							
9. Reichsbahn	860.0	131.0	991.0	601.0	991.0	526.9	991.0
10. Reichspost	77.0	34.0	111.0	95.0	111.0	65.0	111.0
11. Reichsautobahnen	300.0	50.0	350.0	50.0	350.0	3.1	166.0
12 Government Institutions	—	575.0	575.0	165.23	574.9	141.7	431.8
Total B	1237.0	790.0	2027.0	911.2	2026.9	736.7	1699.8
Total A + B	3125.0	1925.0	5050.0	3101.1	4994.0	1591.4	3963.9

Source Bauwirtschaftsbericht 1933, Bauwirtschaftsbericht 1934; Vierteljahrshefte zur Konjunkturforschung (1934), Teil A, S. 70, Wochenbericht des Instituts für Konjunkturforschung (1935) as quoted from Schiller (1936, p. 155)

6 RISK SHARING MACROECONOMIC POLICIES 127

Table 6.5 Projected financial budget of work creation programs on Reich Treasury: 1934–1938 (mil. RM)

Program	1934	1935	1936	1937	1938
Papen Program					
Bill Redemption (incl. related costs)	190	55			
Gereke Sofortprogramm					
Bill Redemption	53	137	137	137	137
Related costs	28	25	17	8	1
First Reinhardt Program					
Bill Redemption	28	243	243	243	243
Related costs	35	40	25	15	50
Second Reinhardt Program					
Subsidies	475				
Tax reimbursement	58	58	58	58	58
Total (Papen, Reinhardt 1 and 2)	867	558	480	461	444
Tax vouchers	312	324	336	348	360
Grand total (Papen and Reinhardt Programs, tax vouchers)	1.179	882	816	809	804

Source In-house report, May 23, 1934 *"Finanziellen überblick über den Reichshaushalt 1934"* Silverman (1998, p. 256, Table 5)

the 1924 Bank Act, the Reichsbank could perform rediscounting of the commercial bills without restrictions.[19] Therefore, the circulation of the bills for drawing, accepting, and discounting was lawful and conceptually permissible from an economic perspective.[20]

The demand for work-creation certificates was immense. Liquidity of the certificates remedied the absence of foreign loans in the capital

---

[19] *"Because the Reichsbank's legitimate function was to finance the real requirements of trade, commerce, and industry, the 1924 law placed no limit on the Reichsbank's discounting of commercial paper. Under the 1924 law, the Reichsbank could participate in the financing of public work-creation programs only by invoking the Reichsbank's unlimited authority to rediscount commercial paper"* (Silverman, 1998, p. 31).

[20] *"In the process they have adopted what, in appearance at least, has been a purely inflationary policy, in as much as* **the money… has been created by the Reichsbank and the banking system in advance of the production of wealth**-*though not, be it noted, in advance of the orders to produce wealth"* (Guillebaud, 1939, p. 214). Because of direct involvement of financial institutions to the pre-financing, therefore, the work-creation bills were *"the most conservative, responsible, temporary means of financing the creation of jobs for Germany's six million unemployed"* (Silverman, 1998, p. 31).

market. The "re-discountable" feature of the certificate satisfied the need for banks and financial institutions that sought "first-class" asset.[21] During the 1920s, banks and financial institutions reaped a substantial gain from liquid assets of foreign capital that dominated the German capital market. However, the crisis and a massive capital flight wiped out all profits and led to the collapse the banking sector. Consequently, the Government imposed strict control on foreign exchange capital to keep certain amount of foreign reserves to stabilize the economy. The Government also blocked transfers of the German currency to maintain internal liquidity. Moreover, the market "benefited" from the Hoover moratorium[22] which increased the liquidity of the capital market. Considering the available liquidity and the need of investors, the capital market absorbed the work-creation bills.

In such a decentralized financing structure, the work-creation bills succeeded in establishing a strong link between the financial and the real sectors of the economy. The bills were neither government subsidy nor debt because they were an off-balance sheet item in the national budget until presented for redemption (Katona, 1936, p. 349). To undertake the Redemption of the bills, two conditions had to be met required (i) economic recovery was strong enough to provide increased revenue to accommodate payments; and (ii) projects financed by the bills had to have been completed (Silverman, 1998, p. 34). When these conditions were met, the government redeemed the bills from holders who requested the payment. Data in Table 6.5 do not reflect the actual money paid for redemption, but reflect the Treasury allocation for the work-creation bills of each fiscal year from 1934 to 1938, if the conditions were satisfied. Related cost was any amount linked to redemption, including reimbursement to participating credit institutions for costs connected with financing the work-creation program.

---

[21] *"The Reichsbank's leading role in financing public work creation programs between 1932 and 1935 took the form of offering rediscount privileges for several types of work-creation bills. The Reichsbank's offer, however, did not necessarily mean that every outstanding bill would be presented to the Reichsbank. It was hoped and expected that, as the economy recovered, banks would view these bills as first-class securities—that is, as securities worth holding in their own portfolios"* (Silverman, 1998, p. 31).

[22] Hoover moratorium, named after US President Herbert Hoover, declared to postpone all payments, both interest and principal, of reparations and war debts for one year period, from December 1931 to 1932. This proposal was intended to ease debtor countries in the midst of the global financial crisis.

The bills distribution plan also demonstrated active participation of private initiative as local enterprises and corporations undertook projects of mutual interest with those associated with a job creation program, such as local governments and communities. After getting approval from the job orderer, these companies issued the bills to the financial market, that is through the banks and financial institutions and capital market, and the latter institutions accepted the bills at discounts. The role of the financial sector became significant since the certificate had to be acknowledged by an appointed public bank with a special mandate to finance public works of different domains:"*Die Deutsche Gesellschaft für Öffentliche Arbeiten A.G.*" (the Oeffa) specialized in financing public utilities; the "*Die Deutsche Bau- und Bodenbank A.G.*" (the Baubo) financed projects for building construction; and "*Die Deutsche Rentenbank-Kreditanstalt*" (the RKA) financed projects for agricultural improvement.

It was mandatory for the bills to carry two signatures: that of the principals (*Die Träger der Arbeit*), and the other of the pre-financing bearer (*Die Träger der Vorfinanzierung*). This acknowledgment was essentially a long-term loan contract, usually from 10 to 25 years' tenor (depending on the probable length of life of the investment), between the principal and the bearer, and served as the source for issuing the commercial certificates that were discountable at German private banks. The principals were entitled to discount the bills at private banks anytime, so long the certificates had yet to mature. The bills theoretically matured after three months, but in practice their redemption was prolonged indefinitely.[23]

Another factor in the success of the bills was the absence of inflation risks. During the experiment, the common fear among economists was that such massive distribution of credit would lead to inflation. This was expected considering the experience with an expansionary monetary policy that led to hyperinflation problem. However, there was no danger of inflation. Richard Ferdinand Kahn, a German-born British economist, remarked that during the time of crisis, monetary expansion for public works would not pose a threat to inflation provided it was accompanied

---

[23] The bills were redeemed if the government viewed that conditions for redemption were satisfied (Army Service Forces Manual M356-5 Civil Affairs, 1944; Guillebaud, 1939, p. 35;).

by an increase in the supply of output from idle resources and unused productive capacity.[24] Furthermore, the work-creation bills and their redemption were linked to the future performance of budget receipts and expenditures. As such, additions to money supply was created commensurate with increase in production. As Baerwald stated: "*The liabilities are so distributed that the annual payments resulting from the guarantee of the Reich do not exceed the possibility of being covered by regular budget receipts*" (Baerwald, 1934, p. 624).

In principle, using the work-creation bills as the means of financing public projects would not lead to inflation if the pace of money supply expanded in tandem with increase in the supply of output. The bills were an instrument for the government to address the problem of fiscal by ensuring that the nominal quantity of money was sufficient to cover the project financing. This is similar to the Friedman rule, which proposes default-free bonds and riskless physical capital, and rate of deflation (or discounting) that eventually will make the nominal interest rate equal to zero (Cole & Kocherlakota, 1998). Reduction in unemployment and expansion of output clearly justified the appropriateness of such policies.

Tax Remission Certificates (Steuergutscheine)

Tax remission certificates were an important instrument of German fiscal policy. Introduced by Chancellor von Papen, it aimed to stimulate private initiatives to invest by remitting payable taxes. Under Hitler, the Government maintained the instrument as a legal fiscal tool for reducing unemployment.[25] The government "rewarded" entrepreneurs and businesses that undertook new capital investments. The mechanism aimed

---

[24] "*If there is in existence a large stock of surplus resources that are not very inferior to the worst of those that are being employed, the elasticity of supply is likely to be very large indeed up to the level of output at which this surplus would be becoming inappreciable. If output is no carried above this level, an expansion of employment bears with it only a very small rise of prices. The greater the depth of the depression, the greater is the expansion of employment that is associated with a given rise in prices. And the greater the expansion of employment that has already been secured by a policy of road-building, the greater is the rise in prices that accompanies a given further expansion of employment; for the short-period supply curve is concave upwards*" (Kahn, 1931, p. 182).

[25] Hitler explained to the Reichstag on the general principle of the law for Removing the Distress of Volk and Reich (*Das Gesetz zur Behebung der Not von Volk und Reich*). He stated: "*The proposed reform of our tax system must result in a simplification in assessment and thus to a decrease in costs and charges. In principle, the tax mill should be built*

6 RISK SHARING MACROECONOMIC POLICIES 131

to induce active public participation in the government program of jobs creation while presenting an indirect means of financing to the governments. Unlike the work-creation bills, "tax remission" did not reflect the critical purpose of the certificates, or the "*raison d'être*" of the instrument. It only indicated their function—or what they offered—as the holders could remit their taxes due at a future date using their certificate.

One distinct feature of the certificates was that it could be pledged for credit or discounted for cash at a small rebate. Entrepreneurs could use this venue to obtain immediate liquidity and used the proceeds for their production expansion. Banks acceptance further enhanced the certificates' attractiveness in the secondary market where holders freely traded it. No tax was imposed on trading this certificate for it enhanced market traceability.

However, two conditions were attached to using the tax remission: First, the authorities distributed the paper between October 1, 1932, and September 30, 1933 only to entrepreneurs or businesses that hired more workers than in the previous quarter of June to August 1932. For each additional worker, the government granted a tax remission certificate worth 100 marks. Corporations that were quick in servicing turnover, ground, and trade taxes were also eligible to attain the certificate because these taxes were related to sales and trading and were remitting the payable tax which would have lowered prices, increased turnover, and recycled for an increase in production. The second condition was associated with time restriction. Treasury only accepted the certificates for the stipulated fiscal year, from April 1, 1934, until March 31, 1939. Katona (1934, p. 33) documented that vouchers distributed from October 1, 1932, to October 1, 1933, were to fall due at any period between 1934 and 1938 at the Treasury. Table 6.6 shows the data of tax remission certificates between 1932 to early 1936.

The characteristics of the tax remission certificates could be summed as follows: For holders, the certificate was a good asset with its value based on the government's liability for a reduction in future tax payment.

---

downstream and not at the source. Because of these measures, the simplification of the administration will certainly result in a decrease in the tax burden..." (Hitler, *Entgegennahmeeiner Erklärung der Reichsregierung*, 23 March 1933, http://www.reichstagsprotokolle.de/Bla tt2_w8_bsb00000141_00036.html). This tax-remission certificate, among others, was one of the economic policies that were kept by the NSDAP government because it aligned with the regime mission to simplify tax system and decrease costs and charges.

132 P. SWASTIKA AND A. MIRAKHOR

Table 6.6 Tax remission certificates (Mil. RM): 1932–1934

Period	Issued[a]	Redeemed[b]	In circulation	Period	Issued	Redeemed	In circulation
1932/10	3	—	3	1934/07	1448.8	8.7	1184.5
1932/11	42.8	—	42.8	1934/08	1455.2	8.4	1182.3
1932/12	263.2	—	263.2	1934/09	1460.2	4.5	1182.6
1933/01	325.7	—	325.7	1934/10	1464.4	3	1183.6
1933/02	391.1	—	391.1	1934/11	1467.9	4.2	1182.7
1933/03	471.9	—	471.9	1934/12	1471.1	2.1	1183.2
1933/04	549.7	—	549.7	1935/01	1472.4	1.5	1182.7
1933/05	644.8	—	644.8	1935/02	1473.4	3.6	1180.1
1933/06	726.6	—	726.6	1935/03	1474.7	1.4	1179.9
1933/07	817.8	—	817.8	1935/04	1475.3	139.4	1041
1933/08	911.6	—	911.6	1935/05	1475.8	83.7	957.9
1933/09	987.8	—	987.8	1935/06	1476	45	913.1
1933/10	1072.7	—	1072.7	1935/07	1476.4	8.4	905
1933/11	1142.1	—	1142.1	1935/08	—	7.4	897.8
1933/12	1215.2	—	1215.2	1935/09	1476.5	1.9	895.9
1934/01	1276.5	—	1276.5	1935/10	1476.6	1.9	894.1
1934/02	1326.3	—	1326.3	1935/11	1476.9	3.7	890.7
1934/03	1362.5	—	1362.5	1935/12	1477.2	0.9	890
1934/04	1395.1	127.9	1263.3	1936/01	1477.3	0.7	889.4
1934/05	1417.8	70.3	1215	1936/02	1477.5	1	888.6

Source Teutul (1962)

[a]Papers in Issuance (Issued): there is no information for August 1935

[b]Papers on redemption (Redeemed): there is no information until March 1934

Because of this quality, the holders could use the paper to obtain direct liquidity, either from banks discounting or traded at the stock exchange for cash.

Though the certificates were classified as Government liabilities, they did not, correspond to debt nor were they like Government bonds. Also, the holders of certificates were not entitled to cash benefit, as the benefit was subject to its submission as a tax rebate. The paper was also not a legal tender, although Treasury accepted the *certificate* as legal means for tax payment. The high or low of the voucher circulation depended highly on public participation in the work-creation program affecting the Government's tax revenue. During the time of growth, this tax voucher contributed to a reduction in the actual tax receipt but not from the accounting standpoint simply because its redemption also represented a decline in liability, composed of tax revenue. It can be reasonably argued also that the instrument differed from subsidy. The tax-remission certificates further emphasized the risk sharing principle in the economic system where Government and the private sector shared the responsibility of financing of the work-creation programs.

MONETARY POLICY: POLICY OF DISCOUNTING

Before 1933, credit expansion was at the heart of German monetary policy. During 1933–1935, however, direct credit expansion assumed a much weaker role as individuals and private sector participated in various public sector projects spurred by Reichsbank's policy of rediscounting commercial papers related to work-creation programs. The chief characteristic of the rediscounting policy was not the act of rediscounting per se but the principle it followed. Rediscounting could be effective only if the additional money supply reached the real sector to finance additional output. The effect of this policy was significant because it ensured stable payment system, especially for suppliers and contractors of the work-creation programs. It also made it possible for the German banks to channel additional money supply directly to principals that undertook to do the projects. This policy revived the financial and the real sectors of the economy.

Such unorthodox monetary policy stance was in sharp contrast to the conventional monetary policy which focused on price stability and maintenance of adequate reserves through implementation of policies that often meant manipulation of the level of money supply. It was also

134   P. SWASTIKA AND A. MIRAKHOR

the conventional prescription that a central bank should undertake a more defensive role in reducing unemployment. These were common principles followed by mainstream monetary authority. The Reichsbank embraced an unorthodox expansionary policy at a time when its reserves were depleted and its position in the global economy weak. The policy displayed a strong commitment to establish a strong link between the financial and the real sector of the economy through implementation of a principle they called "*Mengenkonjunkturstatt Preiskonjunktur*" (*production boom instead of price boom*).[26]

Despite its aggressive policy to support the work-creation programs, the Reichsbank chose to remain autonomous as an independent organization of the State. The Reichsbank kept its control over the monetary policy and enforced a strong discipline in the financial market. All banks and financial institutions had to adhere and support the Reichsbank's efforts in setting up a payment system based on the speed of real sectors activity.

Legal system too supported this policy, which became the foundation of creating an effective financial system, lowering political costs and uncertainty, and ensuring that the parties involved in the work-creation programs complied with the rules of the game. Through discounting the commercial bills of work creation, all additional credits were disbursed for payment of the real sector. This principle was important because it meant it could successfully restore private sector's confidence in banks and financial institutions. This way, financial institutions also shared the burden with the real sector. Moreover, as an immediate impact, discounting liquefied the existing frozen capital and transformed it into working capital for public investments.

The policy stance limited the room for the interest rate to influence the supply and allocation of financial resources. The guarantee of rediscounting had lowered the cost of the transaction to the minimum as the Reichsbank guaranteed the necessary liquidity to back the commercial bills. This system also suppressed the power of rentiers in determining capital allocation. In other words, entrepreneurs and households felt the positive psychological impact of the rediscounting policy as it offered a conducive environment for their participation in providing resources

---

[26] Guillebaud (1939, p. 210) wrote: "*The Germans are fond of the slogan 'MengenkonjunkturstattPreiskonjunktur', by which they mean that their objective is a boom expressed in volume of output and not in value due to price rises*".

6 RISK SHARING MACROECONOMIC POLICIES   135

directly to production. The business also sensed greater certainty as payment for undertaking the projects was assured by this mechanism.

Table 6.7 shows the slowdown in the Reichsbank's rate of discount and a continuous decrease in all market money rates since the end of 1932. This downward evolution reflected a deliberate measure to limit the influence of interest rate on the real economic activity. Interest rate channel thus became far less potent in setting the cost of capital and the price of money.

Guillebaud (1939) pointed out the effect of Dividend Law that regulated the distribution of corporate dividend not to exceed 6%. He suggested that such legal restraint reduced transactions in the Stock Exchange "*except as a market for dealing in old shares*" (Guillebaud, 1939, p. 217).The projects of work-creation programs were devolved to the local communities, excluding the *Autobahn* project, which further discouraged big private lenders from their usual activity.

While the monetary policy of Reichsbank for the period of 1933–1936 deserves a wider discussion, the importance of focusing on discounting policy and not on other components of monetary policy of the Reichsbank was to demonstrate the risk sharing principle behind German economic miracle. The turn of the Central Bank toward concern for

Table 6.7   Interest rates from 1932 to June 1936

Period		*Central Bank discount rate*	*Private discount rate*	*Money for one month*	*Day-to-day money*
1932	January	7	6.94	7.58	7.86
	June	5	4.75	5.76	5.7
	December	4	3.88	5.08	4.91
1933	January	4	3.88	5.03	4.98
	June	4	3.88	5.5	4.93
	December	4	3.88	5.5	4.97
1934	January	4	3.88	4.78	4.74
	June	4	3.76	4.67	4.57
	December	4	3.5	3.56	4.28
1935	January	4	3.51	3.93	3.82
	June	4	3	2.93	3.16
	December	4	3	3.23	2.15
1936	January	4	3	3.09	2.81
	March	4	3	3.07	2.99

Source Board of Governors of The Federal Reserve System (1936)

its social function enabled the institution to restore confidence in the financial market as well as the trust of private sector to support the Government's work-creation policy. As a result, people who were involved in the programs also participated in planning and financing of the projects according to their financial ability.

REFERENCES

Army Services Forces Manual M356-5 Civil Affairs. (1944). *Military government handbook: Germany.*

Baerwald, F. (1934). How Germany reduced unemployment. *The American Economic Review, 24*(4), 617–630.

Board of Governors of the Federal Reserve System. (1936, May). *Federal Reserve Bulletin.*

Cole, H.L., & Kocherlakota, N. (1998). Zero nominal interest rates: Why they're good and how to get them. *Federal Reserve Bank of Minneapolis Quarterly Review, 22*(2), 2–10.

Deutsche Bundesbank (2005). *Deutsches Geld-und Bankwesen 1876 bis 1945. GESIS Datenarchiv, Köln. ZA8222 Datenfile Version 1.0.0.* https://doi.org/10.4232/1.8222.

Feinstein, C. H., Temin, P., & Toniolo, G. (2008). *The world economy between the world wars.* Oxford University Press, Inc.

Grebler, L. (1937). Work creation policy in Germany, 1932–1935 : I. *International Labour Review, 35*, 329.

Guillebaud, C. W. (1939). *The economic recovery of Germany from 1933 to the incorporation of Austria in March 1938.* Macmillan.

Hetzel, R. L. (2002). German monetary history in the first half of the twentieth century. *Federal Reserve Bank of Richmond Economic Quarterly, 88*(1), 1–35.

Hitler, A. (1933a). Aufruf an das Deutsche Volk.

Hitler, A. (1933b, March 23). *Entgegennahmeeiner Erklärung der Reichsregierung.* http://www.reichstagsprotokolle.de/Blatt2_w8_bsb00000141_00036.html.

Katona, G. M. (1934). How real is the German recovery? *Foreign Affairs, 13*(1), 26–44.

Katona, G. M. (1936). The "Miracle" of German recovery. *Foreign Affairs, 14*(2), 348–350.

Overy, R. J. (1975). *German economic recovery.* Clarendon Press.

Schiller, K. (1936). *Arbeitsbeschaffung und Finanzordnung in Deutschland.* Zum Wirtschaftlichen Schicksal Europas: Arbeiten zur deutschen Problematik.

Schmidt, C. T. (1934). *German business cycles 1924–1933*. National Bureau of Economic Research No. 25.

Silverman, D. P. (1998). *Hitler's economy: Nazi work creation programs, 1933–1936*. Harvard University Press.

Teutul, C. (1962). Die Funktion der deutschen Notenbank bei der Staatsverschuldung, Deutsches Reich 1914 bis 1945.

Vossische Zeitung. (1933, June 2). *Das Gesetz Gegen Arbeitslosigkeit. Vossische Zeitung-Morgen Ausgabe*. Berlin.

Wolfe, M. (1955). The development of Nazi monetary policy. *Journal of Economic History, 15*(4), 392–402.

Index

0–1

25 Point Program, 12, 116

A

Acculturation, 68
Accumulation of wealth, 23, 48
Al-Bay', 36–39, 79
Al-Ghazali, 40
Al-Mudawwana al-Kubra, 52
Al-Riba, 36–40, 43
Aquinas, St. Thomas, 73
Aristotle, 3
The Assyrian, 2

B

Bank for International Settlements (BIS), 102
Brüning, Heinrich, 114

C

Cameralwissenschaften, 86
Capital accumulation, 42
Census, 69, 70, 73, 78
Cerati, 51
Column, 51
Commenda, 5, 17, 49–54, 59, 66, 67, 84
Community responsibility, 85
Compagnia, 51
Compera, 70, 71, 78
The Consulato del Mare, 52
Consumption, 10, 18, 24, 25, 29, 30, 32, 44, 64, 103, 104
Coordination, 20, 26, 32, 36, 37, 39, 44, 56, 67, 83, 108, 109
Coordination problem, 32, 44
Corporation, 5, 54, 55, 67, 119
Crédit Mobilier, 18, 43, 60–67, 90, 91

D

Darmstädter Bank, 61, 90, 91
Dawes Plan, 100–102

© The Editor(s) (if applicable) and The Author(s), under exclusive license to Springer Nature Switzerland AG 2021
P. Swastika and A. Mirakhor, *Applying Risk-Sharing Finance for Economic Development*, Political Economy of Islam,
https://doi.org/10.1007/978-3-030-82642-0

140 INDEX

Debt, 1–3, 5–8, 10–13, 23, 25, 26, 28, 32–35, 40, 48, 51, 56, 57, 64, 66–68, 70–72, 76, 79, 93, 95, 100, 102, 103, 106, 108, 109, 119, 128, 133
  artificial recovery, 101
  Dawes Plan, 99
  debt restructuring, 100
  foreign borrowing, 101
  reparation payments, 97, 99–102
  Young Plan, 102
Die Reichsbank, 28
Discounting monetary policy, 133
Dutch United East India Company, 54

E
Economic development, 17, 18, 35, 42, 43, 49, 59, 61, 66, 89, 92
Economic growth, 7, 8, 13, 20, 28, 35, 42, 52, 66, 94, 101, 106, 107, 113
Economic recovery, 18, 29, 105, 128
Economic stability, 8, 14, 35, 36, 54, 60, 62, 69, 95, 100, 101, 106, 133
Efficient monetary system, 94
Entrepreneurial bank, 61
Equity, 5, 11, 35, 38, 56, 57, 59, 62, 88, 90
Esham, 75, 76
Exchange transactions, 34, 107
Expansionary policy, 120, 134

F
Feder, Gottfried, 7–13, 95, 96, 108, 109
Financial crisis, 2, 24, 38, 41, 57, 78, 128
Financialization, 7, 36, 48, 100

financial market, 57, 59, 93, 108, 129, 134, 136
First Reinhardt Program, 123, 127
Fiscal policy, 9, 20, 24, 27, 34, 35, 44, 96, 130
Fisher, Irving, 94, 105
Fraterna, 51
Friedrich List, 87, 88, 103
Full employment, 8, 9, 33

G
Gabella, 71
Genoa, 17, 49, 51, 70, 71, 84
German economy, 7–9, 11–14, 20, 21, 28, 83, 87, 97, 113
Germany, 2, 7, 8, 12, 14, 17–20, 28–31, 72, 83–87, 89, 92, 94, 96, 97, 99–103, 107–109, 113, 121, 127
Germany economic policy
  work-creation programs, 119, 127, 133–135
Gesell, Silvio, 8, 92, 94, 108
Gold standard, 93
Great depression, 28, 83, 103, 105
  unemployment, 7, 9, 13, 18, 20, 32, 41, 44, 102, 103, 106, 113, 114, 117, 118, 123, 124, 130, 134

H
Hansa States, 83
Heimische Kreditexpansion, 104
Helfferich, Karl, 97, 98
Hitler, Adolf, 8, 12, 31, 113, 117, 120, 121, 130, 131
Hoarding, 93, 94, 96, 99, 109
Human development, 35
Hyperinflation, 7, 9, 13, 29, 97, 100, 114, 116, 129

I

Iltizam, 74–78
Incentive, 6, 7, 11, 14, 24, 32, 36, 38, 39, 41, 43, 93
Incentive structure, 6, 14, 36, 39, 43
Industrial capital, 11, 12, 95, 108
Inflation, 8, 13, 18, 30, 32, 96–98, 104, 107, 108, 117, 129, 130
Inflation rate, 30, 96, 107
Interest rate, 1–3, 5, 6, 8, 10–13, 18, 19, 23, 26, 28–35, 37, 38, 40–44, 48, 50, 56, 67, 68, 77–79, 89, 91, 93–95, 101, 103, 104, 106, 108–110, 113, 114, 119, 130, 134, 135
interest slavery, 95
Interest slavery, 108
Intermediary, 60, 65
Investment, 21, 23, 25–27, 30–32, 35, 37, 38, 50, 51, 53–55, 59, 62–64, 66, 89, 101, 109, 121, 124, 129
Islam, 3, 12, 14, 17, 18, 23, 33, 39, 40, 43, 52
Islamic economic, 35
Islamic finance, 12, 20, 23, 33–35, 39, 42–44, 109

J

Joint-stock banks, 49, 60, 67, 90–92, 109
Joint-stock company, 5, 55, 57
Joint-stock system, 55, 56, 58, 59, 65

K

Keynes, John Maynard, 28, 31, 94
Kuala Lumpur Declaration, 33, 39
Kuxen, 85, 86, 107

L

The Late Medieval Commercial Revolution, 49
Lautenbach, Wilhelm, 104
Lex-Mercatoria, 52
Loan capital, 9, 11, 95, 108

M

Macroeconomic policy, 10, 13, 18–20, 26, 29, 44, 113
Malikane, 74
Mammonism, 9
The Maritime Laws of Oleron, 52
Medici Bank, 43
Medieval Christian Europe, 2
Mesopotamia, 1
Modaraba, 17, 39, 52, 66, 109
Monetary policy, 20, 28, 29, 31, 35, 97, 101, 122, 129. *See* 133 –135
Money, 3, 5, 9, 10, 25, 28, 29, 32–35, 39, 40, 44, 50, 51, 60, 61, 72, 75, 78, 88, 89, 91, 93–100, 105, 106, 108, 109, 120, 123, 124, 127–130, 133–135
Monte Vecchio, 71
Motorisierungspolitik, 121, 122
Muhammad Hussein Tabatabai, 36, 40
Musharaka, 17, 39, 66

N

National socialism, 8, 9, 12, 20, 103, 108, 113, 123, 131
The Natural Economic Order, 93
The New Testament, 3
Nine Point Program, 10, 11

O

Ökonomie, 86

142   INDEX

The Old Testament, 3
Ottoman Empire, 42, 47, 73, 74, 78

P

Papiermark, 99
Partnership(s), 2, 5, 34, 38, 39, 42, 43, 48–51, 54, 59, 60, 62, 66, 67, 84, 107, 109
  active partnership, 84
  silent partnership, 84
Polizei, 86
Pre-financing system, 19, 20, 29, 120
Prestiti, 71
Public loan, 78

Q

The Quran, 3, 12, 36, 41, 43

R

Railway notes, 88, 89, 107
Reflationary policy
  Sofort program, 116
Renaissance, 43, 48
Rente, 70, 72, 73, 78
Rentenmark, 98, 99
Rentier(s), 7, 23, 31–33, 40, 48, 72, 93, 94, 108, 134
Risk sharing, 1, 5, 7–10, 12–14, 17–21, 23, 26, 28, 30, 32–39, 42–44, 47, 49, 51, 52, 59, 66, 67, 78, 84, 85, 89, 90, 93, 95, 107–109, 113, 133, 135
Risk-sharing finance, 5, 12, 13, 59
Risk shifting, 2, 6, 8, 21, 23, 33, 35–39, 43, 48, 52, 57, 93
Risk transfer, 1, 2, 5–8, 21, 24, 29, 33–43, 48, 56, 57, 78, 93, 95
Rogadia, 51
Roggenrentemark, 98, 99
Rothschild, 60, 95

S

Saint-Simonian, 64
Salt tax, 71
Saving, 21, 28–30, 33, 37, 44, 55, 77, 92, 106, 107, 120, 124
Schacht, Hjalmar, 8, 28–31, 93, 98, 101
Scholastics, 3
Second Reinhardt Program, 121, 123, 127
Sendegeschäft, 17, 84, 107
Serrata, 53, 67
Social capital, 32, 48, 67
Social justice, 4, 32, 108
Social welfare, 85, 109
Societas, 5, 49, 51, 84
South Sea, 55–57
Speculation, 93–95
Stamp money, 94
  money stamp, 93, 108
Storage costs, 93
The Sumerians, 2

T

Tax-remission certificates, 21, 29, 123, 130–133
Tax system, 78, 130, 131
Timar, 74
Transaction cost, 52, 54, 56, 87, 104, 109
Transitional currency, 98

U

Unemployment, 18, 28, 30, 31, 115, 117, 123
Unterguggenberger, Michael, 105
Usury, 2–4, 56, 69, 72, 73, 79
Utility maximization, 4

V

Valorization, 98

INDEX 143

Venetia, 17, 43, 49–54, 67, 70, 71, 84, 86
Venture capital, 62, 65, 66
von Papen, Franz, 116, 130
von Schleicher, Kurt, 116
Vorfinanzierung, 120, 129

W
Waqf, 42
Wealth inequality, 7, 9, 32, 33
Weimar Republic, 116, 121
Wertbeständiges, 98, 99

Wiederlegung, 84, 107
Wörgl, 104–109
Work-creation bills, 21, 29, 123, 124, 127, 128, 130, 131
Work-creation program, 19, 117, 119
Labour Treasury bills, 118
law against unemployment, 118
Work-notes, 106

Z
Zakat, 18, 42